SOZIOLOGIE

FORUM
DER DEUTSCHEN GESELLSCHAFT FÜR SOZIOLOGIE

Heft 3 • 2024

Herausgeber im Auftrag von Konzil und Vorstand der Deutschen Gesellschaft für Soziologie:
Prof. Dr. Dirk Baecker (verantwortlich im Sinne des Presserechts)
Redaktion: Prof. Dr. Sylke Nissen und Dipl. Pol. Karin Lange, Universität Leipzig, Institut für Soziologie, Beethovenstraße 15, D-04107 Leipzig, Tel.: 0341/97 35 648,
E-Mail: soz-red@sozio.uni-leipzig.de (Redaktion) oder dirk.baecker@zu.de (Dirk Baecker)

Vorsitzende der Deutschen Gesellschaft für Soziologie:
Prof. Dr. Paula-Irene Villa Braslavsky, Ludwig-Maximilians-Universität München,
Institut für Soziologie, Konradstraße 6, D-80801 München
E-Mail: paula.villa@lmu.de, Tel.: 089/2180 2441
Geschäftsstelle der Deutschen Gesellschaft für Soziologie:
Marcel Siepmann (Leitung), DGS c/o Kulturwissenschaftliches Institut Essen, Goethestraße 31, D-45128 Essen, E-Mail: marcel.siepmann@kwi-nrw.de,
Tel.: 0201/1838 138, Fax: 0201/1838 232
Schatzmeisterin der Deutschen Gesellschaft für Soziologie:
Prof. Dr. Heike Delitz, Universität Regensburg, Fakultät Sprach-, Literatur-, Kulturwissenschaft, Altes Finanzamt, Landshuter Str. 4, D-93047 Regensburg, E-Mail: Heike.Delitz@ur.de

Aufnahmeanträge für die DGS-Mitgliedschaft und weitere Informationen unter www.soziologie.de

Die Zeitschrift SOZIOLOGIE erscheint viermal im Jahr zu Beginn eines Quartals. Redaktionsschluss ist jeweils sechs Wochen vorher. Für Mitglieder der DGS ist der Bezug der Zeitschrift im Mitgliedsbeitrag enthalten. Beiträge in der SOZIOLOGIE werden über EBSCOhost Information Services sowie in den Bibliographien von De Gruyter: IBZ und IBR erfasst.

Campus Verlag GmbH, Kurfürstenstraße 49, D-60486 Frankfurt am Main, www.campus.de
Geschäftsführung: Marianne Rübelmann
Programmleitung: Dr. Judith Wilke-Primavesi
Anzeigenbetreuung: Claudia Klinger, Julius Beltz GmbH & Co. KG, Postfach 100154, D-69441 Weinheim, Tel.: 06201/6007-386, E-Mail: anzeigen@beltz.de
Fragen zum Abonnement und Einzelheftbestellungen: Beltz Medien-Service, Postfach 100565, D-69445 Weinheim, Tel.: 06201/6007-330, E-Mail: medienservice@beltz.de

Bezugsmöglichkeiten für Nichtmitglieder der DGS:
Jahresabonnement privat 78 €, Studierende / Emeriti 35 €
Jahresabonnement Bibliotheken / Institutionen 118 € print / 177 € digital (nach FTE-Staffel)
Alle Preise zuzüglich Versandkosten. Alle Preise und Versandkosten unterliegen der Preisbindung. Kündigungen des Abonnements müssen spätestens sechs Wochen vor Ablauf des Bezugszeitraums schriftlich mit Nennung der Kundennummer erfolgen.

Druck: Beltz Grafische Betriebe GmbH, Bad Langensalza
Beltz Grafische Betriebe GmbH ist ein klimaneutrales Unternehmen (ID 15985-2104-1001).
ISSN 0340-918X

MIX
Papier | Fördert gute Waldnutzung
FSC www.fsc.org FSC® C089473

Inhalt

Nachrichten aus der Soziologie

Liebe Kolleginnen und Kollegen,

es ist immer noch Krieg. Doch was ist ein Krieg? Zu Dutzenden, Hunderten, Tausenden sterben die Menschen, Soldaten ebenso wie Zivilisten. Städte werden zerstört, die Erde wird verwüstet, Flüsse werden vergiftet. Soziale Systeme sind irritiert, Netzwerke kämpfen um ihre Identität, Felder sortieren ihre Kräfte. Das Immunsystem der Gesellschaft bekämpft das Nein des Kriegs mit einem Nein zum Krieg. Alle Aufregung in Politik und Öffentlichkeit dient der Unterscheidung des einen Neins vom anderen, doch infiziert vom Krieg sind beide.

Es ist nicht lange her, dass man auch vom Krieg erwartet hat, dass er in einer ›digitalisierten‹ Gesellschaft smarter wird als je zuvor. Präzise und schnelle Eingriffe schalten Kommandozentralen aus, bevor die Truppen auch nur in Bewegung gesetzt werden können. Dem ist jedoch nicht so. Ungeheure Massen an Personal und Material kommen zum Einsatz, ›dumme‹ Bomben töten Zivilisten, Schützengräben werden gegraben, die einen monate- und jahrelangen Belagerungs- und Zermürbungskrieg ankündigen. Natürlich sind auch Drohnen im Einsatz und es werden digitalisierte Daten berechnet. Aber weder im Gazastreifen noch in der Ukraine hätten die Soldaten, Offiziere und Generäle vergangener Kriege Schwierigkeiten sich zurechtzufinden. David J. Betz, *Professor of War in the Modern World* am King's College in London, weist darauf hin, dass ganz im Gegenteil ein schneller Krieg wie der Krieg der USA gegen den Irak im Frühjahr 2003, der nach drei Wochen auch dank der Bestechung irakischer Offiziere durch die CIA entschieden war, das Risiko eingeht, dass der Gegner nicht mitbekommt, dass der Krieg bereits verloren ist. Ohne die Niederlage des Gegners gibt es jedoch auch keinen Sieg des Siegers, wie die bis 2011 währende bürgerkriegsähnlichen Kämpfe irakischer Gruppen untereinander und gegen die Besatzung beweisen. Die Schätzungen ziviler Opfer bis 2011 reichen von Hunderttausend bis zu einer Million Menschen.

Die Nationalismen der modernen Welt dominieren die Kalküle einer digitalisierten Welt. Nicht die Drohung mit einer Steigerung der militärischen Mittel zählt, sondern die schiere Masse an Vernichtung. Und auch Zerstörung, Verwüstung und Tote zählen nicht, solange Systeme, Netzwerke und Kraftfelder intakt sind. Der Krieg endet erst, wenn er unter den Lebenden keinen Rückhalt mehr findet. Aber solange um politischen Einfluss gekämpft wird, militärische Optionen vorhanden sind, Waffengeschäfte gemacht werden, religiöser Eifer eine Chance hat und Massenmedien für Information und Desinformation genutzt werden können, findet der Krieg kein Ende. Die Gesellschaft reproduziert sich auch im Medium des Kriegs. Behörden und Unternehmen, Armeen und Kirchen, Krankenhäuser und Redaktionen arbeiten, solange sich Lebende finden, die sich an der Kommunikation beteiligen, und solange eine Infrastruktur existiert, die diese Kommunikation ermöglicht. Tote werden nicht nur in Kauf genommen, als ›ökologische‹ Effekte in der Umwelt der Systeme hingenommen, sondern von Politik und Militär aktiv produziert. Von »destruktiver Arbeit« sprach Lars Clausen in den 1980er Jahren.

Der Krieg ist das neue Normal. Es ist mit dem alten Normal nicht zu verwechseln. Der Krieg infiziert jede Erwartungsstruktur jeden Systems, jeden Netzwerks und jeden Kräftefelds. Auch wenn man nicht an der Front kämpft und die Kameradinnen und Kameraden neben sich fallen sieht, rechnet man mit Opfern. Jede Kommunikation bekommt diesen zusätzlichen Aspekt, dass sie *noch* möglich ist. Geschickt lenkt die Propaganda einen Großteil der Aufmerksamkeit auf jene, die als Gegner für die Fragilität verantwortlich gemacht werden. Das Gift der einen, die Todesangst, ist das Elixier der anderen.

Es gibt keine Gleichgültigkeit gegenüber den Toten. Sie werden betrauert, verschwiegen und instrumentalisiert. Sie konfrontieren die Gesellschaft mit einem Ende (der Menschen), das (in der Kommunikation) nicht stattfindet. Das ist der Krieg, eine fortgesetzte Produktion (›Autopoiesis‹) von Enden. Könnte man sich den Schmerz und die Trauer eingestehen, ohne zur Rache aufzurufen oder einen Nutzen aus dem Betrieb zu ziehen, der die Toten in Kauf nimmt, wäre man auf dem Weg zu einem Frieden – einem Frieden der Einsicht in die Gefährlichkeit, Unbarmherzigkeit und Brutalität mächtiger Prozesse der Vergesellschaftung.

Mit herzlichen Grüßen
Dirk Baecker

Soziologie, 53. Jg., Heft 3, 2024, S. 271–282

The End of Sociology?

The Analytics of Decline

Juan E. Corradi

»Do not ask what a social phenomenon is.
Ask instead what it is not, and what it is like.«
Everett Cherrington Hughes

When one is trained in the sociology of knowledge, it becomes a habit to carry out research while looking at the same time over one's shoulder, placing the inquiry in a larger context. To use a nautical analogy, the pilot of a boat guides it while practicing situational awareness, above and beyond the most advanced aids to navigation. Over six decades I have practiced teaching and research in sociology and I have observed its relative decline in several nested fields: society at large, the full set of social sciences, and academia.

Sometime ago Volker Meja (a former fellow graduate student at Brandeis University) forwarded to me a journalistic report on a shabby episode in the state of Florida, in an e-mail which he provocatively titled »The End of Sociology?« The article reported a recent decision in Florida to remove »Principles of Sociology« from the state's general education core course options. Undoubtedly this was in consonance with the increasingly belligerent attack by the Governor and his political associates against what they define as a leftist »woke«[1] attempt to indoctrinate students.[2] On the surface this attack

1 Woke is an adjective that refers to a broad awareness of inequality, racial injustice, sexual discrimination, and minority rights. It is often used as a shorthand for some ideas and claims of the American left, like reparation for past black slavery. The catch word is derived from the African American vernacular.

2 For an update and review of the controversy see https://is.gd/UAiz6K. See also the article by Jukka Savolainen (2023). The reaction of the President of the American Sociological Association was not a powerful one, and it reveals that a sociology requirement for

may seem a grotesque repetition – in the American anti-intellectual style – of the ancient criminal allegations against Socrates for »corrupting the youth«. But the comparison would miss the fundamental difference between a »woke« culture that seeks to reinforce preconceived albeit rebellious attitudes and the Socratic method of intellectual discourse that requires the teacher to always assume the role of the devil's advocate in an argument.

In America, direct interference in the academic integrity of an institution is possible in the case of public schools whose budgets are voted by the state legislatures. In other cases, the attack takes place in more circuitous, but no less effective ways, in a sort of a McCarthyistic »un-American activities« accusation by a Republican-dominated lower House of the Congress. The recent forced resignation of two presidents of top elite private universities is an alarming case of political interference in the autonomy and academic integrity of those institutions. The pretext was the vociferous outrage of right-wing legislators at an alleged rampant antisemitism on campus, on the occasion of student protests against the actions of the state of Israel in Gaza, and the accusation that university presidents had »not done enough« to punish such protests.

Those episodes have prompted in me a retrospective look at both the discipline and my own trajectories over sixty years in the field. Whither sociology?

In 1965 I finished in record time my BA degree in sociology at Brandeis University, where I had been recruited while I was a law student in Buenos Aires. A generous scholarship from that institution allowed me to study in the United States. The episode changed my career and my life as well, as I pursued a new intellectual vocation in America during those turbulent years.

In those days Brandeis University was a unique and transformative institution.[3] It was a non-denominational Jewish university founded at the same time as the State of Israel. Among its faculty was a brilliant set of German refugees whose ideas of the social sciences were definitely not in line with the mainstream sociology of the time, whose dominant paradigm was structural functionalism.

---

undergraduates is perhaps also a strategy to mitigate the decline in market share of the discipline within a college (Misra, Carter, Wingfield 2024).

3 For a recollection of the history of Brandeis by one of its founders and long-time president, see Sachar (1976). For a description of Brandeis sociology in the sixties (from a feminist perspective) see Thorne (1997).

Brandeis sociology was heavily influenced by a European outlook, including the critical theory of the Frankfurt School, and also by the field work approach of the Chicago school of sociology. I wrote my undergraduate thesis on the sociological implications of Edmund Husserl's phenomenology, in particular the philosopher's late work on the crisis of European science. My thesis advisors were Kurt H. Wolff, a student of Karl Mannheim and the introducer of Simmel's sociology in the United States, and Herbert Marcuse, who had been a doctoral student of Husserl and Heidegger before the advent of Naziism and of his exile in America.

In 1965 I was pondering whether to embark in further studies in sociology. At the time Herbert Marcuse was forced into retirement (because of age) at Brandeis and moved to California. I fondly remember helping Marcuse pack his books, especially his collection of German classics, including the complete works of Schiller in elegant brown leather binding. I used the opportunity to ask my professor for advice. He invited me to lunch in a French restaurant in Cambridge and then we took a long walk. I remember our conversation on the state of the social sciences in the United States. Regarding my prospects in the discipline, I recall vividly his advice in the form of a warning: »If you choose sociology, it will be either your wedding or your funeral.« He suggested I continued my studies at Brandeis under the guidance of Kurt Wolff but added I could do well in apprenticing to his good friend Barrington Moore, Jr., who was teaching at Harvard in the Russian Research Center and the Department of Government. Later he introduced me to Professor Moore.

I took Marcuse's advice, studied the sociology of knowledge under Wolff at Brandeis, and through an ingenious arrangement also took Moore's graduate seminar on class and politics in the industrial revolution at Harvard's Department of Government, and other courses taught by him in the program of social studies at Harvard College. I thus developed a double interest in the critique of ideology and comparative modern societies in those formative years. It led to a doctoral dissertation on class and politics in the development of Argentina, somewhat pompously titled »Pseudomorphic Modernization« – an adjective borrowed from none other than Oswald Spengler![4]

---

4 Pseudomorphism in geology is the existence of a mineral that has the appearance of another mineral. Spengler used the term to characterize inauthentic cultures shaped by other cultures. In Spengler's words in »Decline of the West«: »By the term ›historical pseudomorphosis‹ I propose to designate those cases in which an older alien Culture lies so

At the time I published my first paper in sociology, co-authored with John David Ober, who had written a dissertation in the history of ideas under Marcuse[5] on the notion of voluntary servitude by Etienne de la Boétie.[6] Our paper was a critique of the ideology implicit in mainstream sociology (Ober, Corradi 1966). It was a critical assessment of sociology in the geopolitical context of the time, marked by the trauma of the Vietnam war.

This early essay on the sociology of sociology delved on the ideological dimensions of what was an accepted paradigm in the field. In the language of Thomas Kuhn, finding the functions of social practices was »normal science« at the time. For Ober and I, what paraded as a paradigm was an idealized model of American society presented as *the* abstract social system (Parsons). For us the critique of ideology was a prelude to discussing methodological alternatives with different premises (e.g. a conflict approach vs. a consensus approach). In other words, we were engaged primarily in a *Methodenstreit*, not in a *Kulturkampf*. We were aware of Max Weber's statement that a socio-critical analysis of thought (as in Marxism) and the relativism of the sociology of knowledge was not a tramway that one could get on and off at will. One's own social position was as determinative or biased as that imputed to another actor. But we believed there were ways of escaping the dilemmas of relativism and of attaining an unattached (*freischwebend*) perspective on ideas in a field of competing perspectives.

In the following decade, the quiet disillusion with the utopian expectations of imminent global change typical of the sixties was accompanied in leading universities by the importation of intellectual currents from Europe and by the cross-fertilization of trends and fashions between the humanities and the social sciences. Structuralism in anthropology, post-structuralism and deconstruction in the literary field (mostly French), converged within sociology with the theme of post-modernity and the reorientation of theory

massively over the land that a young Culture, born in this land, cannot get its breath and fails not only to achieve pure and specific expression-forms, but even to develop fully its own self-consciousness. All that wells up from the depths of the young soul is cast in the old moulds, young feelings stiffen in senile works, and instead of rearing itself up in its own creative power, it can only hate the distant power with a hate that grows to be monstrous.« (Spengler 1961: 263; see also Corradi 1974)

5 Marcuse taught in the Program on the History of Ideas at Brandeis.

6 »Discours de la servitude volontaire« is an essay by Étienne de La Boétie, Michel de Montaigne's closest friend, published clandestinely in 1577. This short text, composed when the author was only 18, has made the rounds through the centuries and is relevant even today (de La Boétie 2010).

in diverse directions – Marxism, psychoanalysis, linguistics, and phenomenology among them. Experimentation with new approaches to the study of knowledge, power, and justice, and inter-disciplinarity, were in some quarters the order of the day. Sociology lost a unitary theoretical framework and was rent asunder by competing paradigms, often deaf to each other's claims.[7]

After the continuation for some time of both growth and salience inside the discipline and of its position in the larger academic field,[8] some symptoms of decomposition and decline set in. These became manifest in the critique of the discipline uttered by Lewis Coser[9] from the »cockpit« of the profession. In his 1975 presidential address to the American Sociological Association he lamented the consequences of two then-prevailing trends: the fetishism of statistical methods on the one hand, and sectarian esoteric intellectual cults[10] on the other (Coser 1975).

In his view both impeded the creative growth of the discipline. In their own ways, each led to the abandonment of substantive areas of inquiry in favor of linguistic or mathematical virtuosity. Coser was no stranger to the sociology of knowledge (Coser 1966) but he came short of analyzing the totality of the academic field and the shifting situation of sociology within it. This kind of analysis was being developed at the time in France by Pierre Bourdieu. The latter combined the immanent and internal interpretation of the discipline with its position in a larger context of power relations.[11]

From a Bourdieuan perspective Coser's warnings were a good preliminary step in a serious diagnosis of the evolution of the discipline. He was right in suspecting that methodological prowess bereft of a solid theoretical base is like a Pirandellian character in search of an author – something like the skill of a good plumber that can be applied to a number of practical issues or problems outside as well as inside the discipline. And Coser's critique of self-regarding and sectarian paradigms was also right: They made the discipline appear less respectable in front of others within the academy. Moreover, some of its erstwhile substantive research areas in domains like

7 There were attempts to synthesize the various approaches, as in the work of Antony Giddens, but they generally did not go beyond a fashion parade.

8 The late sixties and early seventies were perhaps the apex of the golden age of sociology in the West.

9 One of my Brandeis teachers in the early sixties.

10 He singled out ethnomethology at the time.

11 Cf. Bourdieu's contributions to the journal *Actes de la Recherche*, and eventually his book, »Homo Academicus« (1984).

large power structures, comparative socio-economic development, and global conflict (concerns of classical sociology) began to migrate to other disciplines like economics, political science, anthropology, and history. In those areas of inquiry sociology had less to say than it had before.

In a Bourdieu-style mapping of the academic field sociology moved down from a central to a peripheral position within the academy and away from an interface with socially strategic partners in the wider field of power in society and towards occasional partnerships with unstable ideological and social movements. In short, it moved from being a big fish in a small pond to a smaller fish in a larger one.

Twenty years after Coser's warnings, Irving Louis Horowitz produced a more dire diagnosis. His vehemence in the critique of his own discipline, as it had evolved in those two decades may sound familiar to the student of religious movements: It has the shrill tone of an apostate (on the right) who was once an apostle (on the left). Nevertheless, Horowitz pointed to the deleterious effects of sectarian advocacy for the objectivity of the profession. He detected an encroachment of »progressive« dogmatism in sociological studies designed to confirm pre-established suppositions (derived from a skeletal Marxism) and above all, in the analysis of society at large, the focus on the trees at the expense of the forest – exactly the opposite tack of the grand tradition of the founders. In one area after another, Horowitz showed how this same formulaic thinking dominated the field, resulting in a crude reductionist view of contemporary social life, out of step with social change itself (Horowitz 1994).

In all fields of inquiry, evolution leads to specialization, to the point that practitioners in one subfield are likely to interact with other disciplines more often than with members of other subfields in their own discipline. In the case of sociology the single paradigm of early days (as in Parsonsian structural functionalism) that for all its scholasticism[12] kept it aloof from ideological conflicts in the wider field of societal power, gave way to a multiplication of perspectives, often esoteric and faddish, and sometimes sporting the name of »theory« without scientific rigor. Sometimes it is difficult to distinguish genuine specialization from ad hoc fragmentation, for instance research on social inequality from grievance studies.

12 See Sztompka (1971) and especially the early critique by Barrington Moore, Jr. (1953). Among Marxists, an equivalent scholasticism was evident in the work of Louis Althusser and his disciples, notably Marta Harnecker in Latin America.

In my days at NYU, especially the 1990s, and harking back to my experience at Brandeis, I sought to broaden the intellectual horizons of sociology on campus by launching a series of mini-seminars on European Sociology with my friend and colleague Wolf Heydebrand. For the two of us and very few others[13] the series was a feast. But for local sociologists the mini-series went almost unnoticed, with rare exceptions tied to some recognizable names: Alain Touraine, Michel Crozier, Pierre Bourdieu, Cornelius Castoriadis, Antony Giddens, Niklas Luhman, Zygmunt Bauman, David Frisby, Jacques Leenhardt, among them.[14] I think however that they left no significant mark in the thought or research of the Department.

The marginalization of this and other efforts in my own department prompted me to »bail out« in the most elegant way I could. I strengthened intellectual alliances with colleagues in the departments of French Studies, History, and Anthropology, and made a few career moves that proved attractive. One was to become a Dean in the Graduate School of Arts and Science, first under a brilliant anthropologist – Annette Weiner – and then all by myself, dealing with the good and the bad not of one department any more but of forty six; the other was to join Richard Sennett – a real public intellectual with a foot in NYU – in the creation of a university-wide Committee on Theory and Culture; and finally to move to Europe directly as Executive Director of New York University in Florence.

In all of these venues I felt that I could breathe a broader air. When that was not enough, I ventured in ocean sailing on my own boat and crossed the Atlantic four times at the helm of a small sailing vessel, with my wife Christina Spellman, also a sociologist (art and urban studies). Sailing was my avocation and an antidote to the petty politics of the university. In some ways this venture into world sailing was a compensation for the failures and frustrations in the political micro-cosmos of academia.

I would have liked to stay in Florence – the city of Machiavelli – at the helm of a great institute of European-American Relations, a sort of Davos not in the Alps but in the Tuscan hills. It was not to be, as my bosses at NYU preferred to keep the Florence campus as one more of the many study

---

13 Some from other departments and some brilliant outsiders like Paul Piccone, editor of the critical journal *Telos*, and occasionally Wolfgang Schivelbusch – both friends of mine that were rare *freischwebende* intellectuals in New York.

14 Jürgen Habermas was more influential elsewhere, as a frequent visiting scholar at The New School for Social Research, physically close to NYU, but intellectually much closer to the legacy of the Frankfurt School.

abroad programs in that city, catering mostly to undergraduates. My ambitions were thwarted, even though the Florentine experience was rewarding in many other ways. Eventually I produced a novel on the life of Florence as I witnessed from my perch (Corradi 2021). I decided to leave at the end of the millennium, do more ocean sailing, and retool my intellectual kit, focusing on comparative studies and geopolitics.

One thing I kept from my Florentine experience, for which an anecdote will suffice. In 1998 I was graciously allowed by the Mayor of Florence to spend time alone in an area of the Palazzo Vecchio normally closed to the public: the study of Nicolò Machiavelli. There I reflected on the analysis that the great political thinker made when forced into exile – bad for him but good for posterity – on the basic questions that to this day inform political sociology and geo-politics, to wit: Who rules? How does a ruler manage power? Who is afraid of what?[15]

Of particular interest for me was the role of fear in political and social life. In the 1990s, and on the occasion of studying the military regimes of South America in a recent past, I led a collective study on the uses of fear (in its extreme form, terror) by such regimes. It resulted in a volume titled »Fear at the Edge«, sponsored by the Social Science Research Council of the United States (Corradi, Weiss Fagen, Garreton 1992). It has been my most cited study in the field, and made me a pioneer in the sociology of fear. Eventually this interest of mine morphed into an inquiry into the sociology of conflict and war – a novelty in my own department, which graciously allowed me to indulge in these topics, though not considering them important enough for the curriculum.

When I returned to the New York campus in 2002 the world had changed; the university had changed; and I had changed. Although I came back to the Department of Sociology, now renewed under the capable leadership of Craig Calhoun, I shifted my research and teaching interests to international politics. Starting with courses and seminars on comparative modern societies, I continued to pursue my interest in the sociology of conflict and war, and finally and directly, to delving in geo-politics proper, where I continue to these days.

15 For a seminal presentation of what is at stake, and in the vein of Machiavelli (although he does not mention the illustrious Florentine) it is useful to consider the text of Max Weber's lecture in Munich addressed to a young audience of distraught demobilized soldiers in 1919, »Politics as a Vocation« (Politik als Beruf; Weber 1988).

Classical theorists[16] are always mentioned with reverence, but their progeny is heterogeneous and lacking in equivalent stature. In the domain of theory, sociology resembles in some ways an orphan brought up by its grandparents. One famous dictum by a great mathematician (Alfred North Whitehead) comes immediately to mind: »A science which hesitates to forget its founders is lost.« And sociology hesitates a lot.

Claudio Benzecry and Monika Krause, two of the most accomplished academic sociologists produced by my own department at NYU in recent years have published an important text (a collective volume) that seeks to take stock with – as the title indicates – social theory now (Benzecry, Krause, Reed 2017). They note fragmentation in this domain, and an active exchange or »trading« with other intellectual domains. That is expressed in the difficult distinction, if not indistinction, between *social* and *sociological* theory. The organizers of this volume try heroically to find a focus, or at least foci, as substitutes for a productive paradigm in the discipline. The connection of the various theories (*theoretical perspectives* is a better term) with empirical research remains tenuous. The latter continues to develop as a theoretically unmoored technology. Moreover, the arena of loosely denominated »theories« has a fluid connection with non-scientific social movements, with their literature and slogans in the wider society. If I search for a reasonably precise definition of any of these »theories« I find a mumbo-jumbo of perspectives stemming from a variety of sources.[17]

On the hinge between the academic and the non-academic world stands the ambiguous figure of the public intellectual. Some sociologists attained this status in America, but most of them in Europe, especially in France, and some of them late in life like Norbert Elias and Zygmunt Bauman. Those in France were called *maîtres à penser* or more generally *philosophes*. While these individuals sometimes called attention to sociology in the mass and later social media, they often also simplified or distorted concepts and findings and straddle cavalierly different fields of knowledge. For some the job was not the advance of knowledge, but the *alegato pro domo suo* (calling media attention to self) and the cry of *J'accuse!* inaugurated by Emile Zola, and thereafter

16 The brightest stars in this constellation have been Marx, Weber, Durkheim, with lesser ones like Simmel and Mannheim among them.

17 An example: »Queer theory's origin is hard to clearly define, since it came from multiple critical and cultural contexts, including feminism, post-structuralist theory, radical movements of people of color, the gay and lesbian movements, AIDS activism, many sexual subcultural practices such as sadomasochism, and postcolonialism.« https://guides.library.illinois.edu/queertheory/background. Last retrieval on May 22, 2024

mostly a sort of shadow boxing parading as militancy. Sometimes it was hard to disentangle researcher from publicist, concept from slogan, sociological terms from terms in other fields, and all these from common conversation.[18]

Of the most brilliant public intellectuals I met or worked with some were bona fide sociologists: Roland Barthes, Michel Foucault, and Alain Touraine[19] were a source of inspiration. Pierre Bourdieu, a sociologist whom I admired and frequented, attained stardom too. He was a sociological research machine all of his own and left his mark for quite some time in the field. But the heyday of *maîtres à penser* came to an end with the new millennium, followed by more technical, anonymous, and team-based research.

On the practical side, the job prospects of sociology graduates in America are not too bad in relation to other social sciences. Unemployment rates (relatively high but below 10 percent) are evenly spread across economics; political science and government, and sociology. A noticeable difference is that among graduate students in the discipline the preferred career is academic. Sociology has a larger share of new doctoral recipients employed in the academy than any of the other scientific fields and this situation has not changed much over the last two decades. Its survival hinges a lot on close circuit reproduction.

Considering other career paths, we see that the alternatives to academic life are not lacking. However, when one looks at these careers one finds that they are far from the cutting edge: They are by and large ancillary positions in the middle to lower ranks of government and social services. To put it grossly, the field operates less in the production of significant new knowledge than in the reproduction of the administrative state. I should not expect any great intellectual innovation in such areas of activity. The picture is one of a field with relatively stable but mediocre prospects. In my own experience at New York University the most brilliantly successful alumni are those who left the field altogether – though perhaps not all of its teachings – for careers in business and finance. A few do well in academia. But there is no breakthrough – no theoretical leap, and no discovery of note. And so the field continues on its path of conventional studies, with some developments

18 I can cite the following comment as an illustration: »In the weeks after Hamas's brutal Oct. 7 attack in Israel and Israel's brutal response, as the world tried to make sense of the violence and its origins, the language of postcolonialism suddenly seemed ubiquitous, even in mainstream conversation: The terms ›decolonization‹, ›settler-colonialism‹ and ›empire‹ appeared regularly not just on social media but also in newspapers and on podcasts.« Max Strasser (2024) on Adam Shatz.

19 Touraine was the sole sociologist in this trio.

in quantitative and qualitative studies – in that order – but without much bang for the buck.

At this point in my career, upon retirement and after joining the ranks of the »emeritocracy«, I have continued doing research and writing in the domain of geo-politics, producing several books. An incurable writer, I also produced a tome on something else, namely a book on sailing which made quite a splash in nautical circles, and I wrote a novel too.

Returning to the initial and provocative question that prompted these recollections, I have written numerous articles on the international situation in our troubled times. They are informed by sociology but not squarely in the field, because I find the latter quite somnambular in the understanding of international affairs. They are published in an internet journal that appears in three languages, *Opinión Sur.*[20] At some point, their collection might see the light of day in the form of a book. I wish to publish this in Spanish first, as a sort of homecoming, in a way, to my Ithaca in this odyssey – my native Argentina.

In closing I realize that I have come full circle in a sketchy outline of what is not an auto-biography but an auto-ethnography. In 1897, Mark Twain, upon reading his obituary, is said to have remarked, »The reports of my death are greatly exaggerated.« In 2024, to the question posed in the title, the proper answer is, in my view, »sociology is alive but not too well«. It muddles through, while some practitioners still wait for a breakthrough.

References

Benzecry, Claudio E. / Krause, Monika / Reed, Isaac Ariail (eds.) 2017: Social Theory Now. Chicago: The University of Chicago Press

Bourdieu, Pierre 1984: Homo Academicus. Paris: Les Editions de Minuit.

Corradi, Juan E. 1974: Pseudomorphic modernization: class and politics in Argentine development. Ann Arbor, Mich.: University Microfilms International.

Corradi, Juan E. 2021: Innocents Abroad. Meadville, PA: Fulton Books.

Corradi, Juan E. / Weiss Fagen, Patricia / Garreton, Manuel Antonio (eds.) 1992: Fear at the Edge. State Terror and Resistance in Latin America. Berkeley: University of California Press.

Coser, Lewis A. 1966: Men of Ideas: A Sociologist's View. Glencoe, Ill.: The Free Press.

---

20 https://opinionsur.org.ar/wp/?lang=en.

Coser, Lewis A. 1975: Presidential Address: Two Methods in Search of a Substance. American Sociological Review, vol. 40, no. 6, 691–700.

de La Boétie, Étienne 2010 [1577]: Discours de la servitude volontaire. Bordeaux: Ed. Mille et une nuits.

Horowitz, Irving Louis 1994: The Decomposition of Sociology. New York: Transaction Books.

Misra, Joya / Carter, Prudence / Wingfield, Adia Harvey 2024: Removing sociology as a Florida core course demonstrates the danger of politicizing education. Tampa Bay Times, February 1. https://www.acls.org/news/american-sociological-association-speaks-out-on-floridas-removal-of-sociology-as-a-course-option, last retrieval on May 22, 2024.

Moore, Barrington 1953: The New Scholasticism and the Study of Politics. World Politics, vol. 6, no. 1, 122–138.

Ober, John David / Corradi, Juan E. 1966: Pax Americana and Pax Sociologica: Remarks on the Politics of Sociology. Catalyst (Summer), 41–54.

Sachar, Abraham L. 1976: A Host at Last. Boston: Little, Brown and Co.

Savolainen Jukka 2023: Florida's Shunning of Sociology Should Be a Wake-Up Call. The field has morphed from scientific study into academic advocacy for left-wing causes. The Wall Street Journal, December 7, 2023. https://www.wsj.com/articles/floridas-shunning-of-sociology-should-be-a-wake-up-call-curriculum-higher-education-politics-0fdbd542, last retrieval on May 22, 2024.

Spengler, Oswald 1961: The Decline of the West. Abriged translation. London: George Allen & Unwin Ltd.

Strasser, Max 2024: Opinion Today. The New York Times, February 5, 2024.

Sztompka, Piotr 1971: The logic of functional analysis in sociology and social anthropology. Quality & Quantity, vol. 5, no. 2, 369–388. https://doi.org/10.1007/BF00218989.

Thorne, Barrie 1997: Brandeis as a generative institution: Critical perspectives, marginality, and feminism. In Barbara Laslett / Barrie Thorne (eds.), Feminist Sociology: Life Histories of a Movement. New Brunswick, NJ: Rutgers UP, 1–27.

Weber, Max 1988 [1919]: Politik als Beruf. In Max Weber, Gesammelte Politische Schriften. Herausgegeben von Johannes Winckelmann, 5. Auflage, Tübingen: Mohr, 505–560.

Soziologie, 53. Jg., Heft 3, 2024, S. 283–304

Soziologische Spuren im Verschwörungsdenken

Georg Vobruba

»Und was das Schlimmste daran war:
Er glaubte seine Lügen gar!«
Erich Kästner (1932)

1. Gewisse Ähnlichkeiten

Die Soziologie und das Verschwörungsdenken haben etwas gemeinsam. Beide setzen bei Beobachtungen der sozialen Verhältnisse an, interpretieren sie und bieten Wissensbestände über die Gesellschaft. Ihre Interpretationen unterscheiden sich allerdings diametral. Damit stellen sich zwei Fragen. Worauf sind die fundamentalen Unterschiede zurückzuführen? Und wo finden sich dennoch Spuren von Soziologie im Verschwörungsdenken?

Luc Boltanski (2013) hat auf gewisse Ähnlichkeiten zwischen Soziologie und Verschwörungsdenken aufmerksam gemacht. Wir können ihm darin folgen, dass er ihre Grundlage im gemeinsamen historischen Entstehungskontext sieht, nämlich in der Lösung des Realitätsverständnisses von transzendentalen verursachenden Kräften und der Freisetzung von Möglichkeiten zu intensiveren innerweltlichen Warum-Fragen als Folge. Dafür spricht auch der gemeinsame Zeitraum ihrer Entstehung, die zweite Hälfte des 19. Jahrhunderts. Boltanskis Beobachtung ist höchst anregend, seine Interpretation bleibt aber zu undifferenziert, indem er grosso modo die Suche nach Beziehungen zwischen sozialen Entitäten als die Ursache der Ähnlichkeiten anführt. Es ist klar, dass sich aus einem so weiten Verständnis von Kausalität eine große Schnittmenge von Verschwörungsdenken und Soziologie ergibt. Dass dies in die Irre führt, lässt sich erkennen, sobald man Kausalität schärfer fasst; und zwar in einer grundlegenden, aber im Prinzip einfachen Weise:

Meine folgenden Überlegungen beruhen auf der Unterscheidung zwischen dem traditionalen Weltbild und dem Weltbild der Moderne, beziehungsweise auf deren unterschiedlichen Logiken, der traditional absolutistischen Logik und der modernen relationalen Logik (Dux 2017; Vobruba 2019: 14 ff.). Diese beiden Logiken legen zwei grundsätzlich unterschiedliche Modi fest, in denen Warum-Fragen beantwortet werden, und folglich zwei unterschiedliche Verständnisse von Kausalität. In der traditional-absolutistischen Logik führen Warum-Fragen zurück auf einen absoluten Bezugspunkt, der immer schon vorausgesetzt, nicht anzweifelbar und nicht überprüfbar ist. In der modern-relationalen Logik führen Warum-Fragen in Verweisungszusammenhänge; das Fragen geht grundsätzlich immer weiter und ist nur durch ein klar formuliertes Beweisziel abschließbar.

Die Soziologie dachte von ihren Anfängen an in dem Sinn modern, dass sie ihre Wissenschaftlichkeit auf Beobachtungen gründete, doch konnte sie den vormodernen Denk-Rahmen noch nicht aufbrechen, in den sie ihre Einsichten einfügte. Unverkennbar ist das im »Cours de philosophie positive«, den Auguste Comte zwischen 1830 und 1842 verfasste (Comte 1933). Comte will die Philosophie, »befreit von der Metaphysik ebenso wie von der Theologie« (ebd.: 519), auf die »positive Methode« verpflichten, die auf »der Unterordnung der Einbildungskraft unter die Beobachtung« beruht (ebd.: 79). Aber er baut sie dann doch in die zwangsläufige Abfolge seines Dreistadiengesetzes und damit in eine Konstruktion spätmetaphysischer Geschichtsphilosophie ein (Wagner 2001: 37 ff.). Die Geschichte der Klassiker danach, vor allem Emile Durkheim, Ferdinand Tönnies, Max Weber und Karl Mannheim, lässt sich als fortgesetzte Anstrengungen lesen, die Reste traditional-absolutistischen Denkens im Fach abzuschütteln. Analog finden sich in der Philosophie Übergangsschritte, die bezeichnender Weise zugleich eine gewisse Bewegung der Philosophie in Richtung Sozialwissenschaften sind. Insgesamt führt die Auflösung des traditional-absolutistischen Rahmens wissenschaftlichen Denkens zur Ausdifferenzierung der Wissenschaften als einem Moment der sich zunehmend entfaltenden funktional differenzierten kapitalistischen Gesellschaft, in der das Störpotential des ökonomischen Systems für andere Systeme ihm seine relative Dominanz sichert. (So, zögerlich, Luhmann 2005: 270; vgl. Schimank 2015)

Das Verschwörungsweltbild dagegen wird von dem Versuch dominiert, die vormodern-absolutistische Logik gegen die Moderne zu behaupten und gegen die Moderne zu denken (Vobruba 2024a). Erklären im Rahmen des

Verschwörungsweltbildes geht von der Voraussetzung aus, dass eine mächtige Gesellschaftsspitze die sozialen Verhältnisse nach ihrem Willen gestaltet. Zum Beispiel: »Alles, was jetzt passiert, ist Teil des Rockefellers-Plan der 1950er Jahre, die Weltherrschaft zu übernehmen.«[1] Diese Logik der Welterklärung hat mehrere Implikationen: Die Interpretation folgt strikt der Logik der Handlung. Was der Fall ist, ist von der mächtigen Gesellschaftsspitze so gewollt. Intentionen führen zu den ihnen entsprechenden Effekten, und von den Effekten lässt sich auf entsprechende Intentionen zurückschließen. Darum hat man mit den Verursachern zugleich die Schuldigen gefunden. Die Gesellschaft ist strikt manichäisch geordnet: Die kleine Gruppe der »Supermächtigen«,[2] der Gesellschaftsgestalter, steht der großen Mehrheit gegenüber, denen die herrschenden Verhältnisse aufgenötigt werden. Im Verschwörungsweltbild führen alle Warum-Fragen zurück zu den Supermächtigen als dem absoluten Anfang aller Erklärungen.

Das Verschwörungsdenken bewegt sich im Rahmen der absolutistischen Logik des vormodernen Weltbildes, beansprucht aber, die Gesellschaft der Moderne kritisch und in Hinblick auf fundamentale Veränderungen zu interpretieren (Vobruba 2024a: 120 ff.) Daraus resultiert eine spezifische Dynamik. Die Unvereinbarkeit von absolutistischer Theoriekonstruktion mit der modernen, funktional differenzierten Gesellschaft führt zu Interpretationsproblemen, die im Rahmen der Logik des Verschwörungsweltbildes immer wieder intentionalistisch aufgelöst werden müssen: Mainstream-Fakten, die verschwörungsdenkerischen Auffassungen entgegenstehen, können nur als Lügen der Supermächtigen und ihrer Handlanger verstanden werden.

Ich werde im Folgenden soziologische Spuren im Verschwörungsweltbild suchen; und zwar entlang einer Skizze, wie das Verschwörungsweltbild seine selbsterzeugten Probleme bearbeitet und sie dadurch immer weiter ins Grundsätzliche verschiebt, bis das Verschwörungsweltbild samt jeglicher Wirklichkeit sich selbst verliert.

1 Uncut news 16.4.2024. Für eine kurze Beschreibung der hier verwendeten Internetquellen vgl. Vobruba (2024a: 9 ff.). Alle Verweise wurden zuletzt am 26. April 2024 geprüft.

2 Die Besetzung der Position ist relativ beliebig. Es werden dafür bekannte reiche Personen (Bill Gates, George Soros) oder Familien (Rothschild, Rockefeller), transnationale Institutionen (WHO, UNO) und immer wieder auch Chiffren wie »die Ostküste«, »die Hochfinanz« verwendet.

2. Es gibt für alles *eine* Ursache

»Schockmomente« (James 2022) wie die internationale Finanzkrise samt Eurokrise, Flüchtlingsströme, Corona-Pandemie, Pandemiepolitik und Kriege lassen sich nicht an den Rand des individuellen Erfahrungshorizonts abdrängen, sondern involvieren Mehrheiten im globalen Westen unmittelbar materiell und moralisch. Der daraus entstandene Begriff »Polykrise« erklärt zwar nichts, drückt aber ein Gefühl umfassender Unsicherheit aus: Soziale Komplexität überwältigt die individuellen Lebenswelten. Eine Reaktion darauf ist die Suche nach Übersichtlichkeit. Das Verschwörungsweltbild verspricht, eine einfache Ordnung in die verstörende Komplexität der Welt zu bringen. Es interpretiert die sozialen Verhältnisse als Inszenierung einer abgehobenen Elite, der Supermächtigen, die auf Vermehrung ihres Reichtums und ihrer Macht aus sind. Das ist die *eine* Erklärung für alles.

Das Verschwörungsweltbild überträgt die Handlungslogik des Alltagsdenkens auf komplexe Zusammenhänge (Vobruba 2024b: 82 f.). Das bedeutet, die soziale Welt und alles in ihr auf die Intentionen eines mächtigen Handlungszentrums zurückzuführen. Dieser absolute Bezugspunkt von Welterklärung steht immer schon fest, und da in erster Linie Unglück erklärungsbedürftig ist (»why do bad things happen to good people?«), steht auch fest, dass das Handlungszentrum böse ist. Alle Rückfragen nach Ursachen führen also zu den bösen Intentionen der Supermächtigen, die die Welt beherrschen. *Sie* wollen *Uns* kontrollieren, manipulieren, enteignen, ausrotten. Die ultimative Frage lautet: »I've always wondered how it works. The Rothschilds, Soros, Klaus Schwab and co … do they communicate directly with demons, fallen angels, Lucifer even ?? how did they become so evil ?«[3] Die Logik des Verschwörungsweltbildes legt die Antwort immer schon fest: Ja, jene Supermächtigen sind böse, weil sie ihre Befehle direkt vom Bösen selbst erhalten. Spätestens bei ihm endet das Warum-Fragen, denn die Bösheit des Bösen muss und kann nicht weiter begründet werden. Es ist in sich böse. Keine weiteren Fragen. Die Befehlskette im Verschwörungsweltbild ist also klar: Möglicherweise hat der Satan die Supermächtigen in der Hand, ganz sicher aber haben sie die Politiker unter Kontrolle. Illustrationen dieser Vorstellung zeigen stereotyp Marionetten. Man sieht die Schnüre, an denen sie hängen, man sieht lenkende Hände, man sieht aber nie die Puppenspieler: Die oberste Lenkungsinstanz bleibt im Dunklen. Eine Ausnahme bilden

3 Aus einem Kommentar zum Text von Brandon Smith, *Rothschild Admits ESG Failure As Globalists Shift To »Inclusive Capitalism« Agenda.* Alt-Market 13.9.2023.

antisemitische Darstellungen »jüdischer Weltherrschaft«. Die Besetzung des mächtigen Handlungszentrums ist in diesem Fall offensichtlich.

Das Verschwörungsdenken wendet sich gegen ein Kernmerkmal der Moderne, ihre Komplexität. In komplexen sozialen Verhältnissen lassen sich Intentionen in aller Regel *nicht* 1 : 1 realisieren. Im Verschwörungsweltbild dagegen folgt alles den Absichten der bösen Macht. Was war die Corona-Pandemie? Eine von langer Hand geplante Verschwörung gegen die Menschheit. Was sind Finanzkrisen? Tricks, mit denen die Reichen sich noch reicher und *uns* arm machen. Kriege? Inszenierungen, um die Agenda der Supermächtigen durchzusetzen. Wahlen? Inszenierte Täuschungsmanöver. Die Umweltkrise? Globale Erwärmung? Täuschungen, um die Weltbevölkerung zu reduzieren. Und soziale Komplexität selbst: ein »Versklavungstrick«[4] der Supermächtigen, der ihnen das Herrschen erleichtert (Vobruba 2024a: 157 ff.). Das Verschwörungsweltbild bietet Erklärungen, die in ihrer Logik zwar konsistent sind, die aber andauernd mit der Mainstream-Wirklichkeit kollidieren. Diese Kollisionen müssen irgendwie abgearbeitet werden. Das verursacht Folgeprobleme.

3. Viele Lügen

Was tun, wenn die Mainstream-Wirklichkeit der eigenen Sicht der Dinge diametral entgegensteht? Im Verschwörungsweltbild gibt es nur eine Reaktion: Es werden nicht die Deutungen revidiert, sondern Tatsachen in Frage gestellt. Man behauptet, dass der Mainstream lügt, und entwirft Gegenwahrheiten. Wer ist der Mainstream? Im Verschwörungsweltbild sind das so gut wie alle. Politik und Medien sind von den Supermächtigen gekauft, ebenso die Wissenschaften samt ihren »notorisch lügenden Professoren«.[5] Es gibt die »Gas-Lüge«, die »Klima-Lüge« und die »Corona-Lüge, die größte Propagandanummer der Weltgeschichte«.[6] Und so weiter. »Wir werden ständig bestohlen, betrogen und verarscht.«[7] Der Lügenvorwurf ist rasch erhoben, aber man begibt sich damit in eine soziale Konstellation mit einer eigenen Dynamik, die sich kaum beherrschen lässt.

---

4 Hans-Jürgen Geese, *Der Todeskampf des Kapitalismus.* Uncut news 12.6.2023.
5 Walter van Rossum, *Die Fälschung der Welt.* Manova 5.10.2023.
6 Anselm Lenz, *Die neue deutsche Demokratiebewegung.* Manova 19.3.2024.
7 *Christine Lagarde: Inflation hängt mit dem Klimawandel zusammen.* Uncut news 18.12.2023.

Die Lüge ist »eine Irrtumserregung«, die darin besteht, »daß der Lügner die wahre Vorstellung, die er besitzt, dem Anderen verbirgt« (Simmel 1992: 388). Die soziale Konstellation der Lüge impliziert also, dass eine Behauptung nicht zutrifft, dass vielmehr etwas anderes zutrifft, dass der Lügner dies weiß und die Belogene es nicht weiß, und dass der Aufdecker der Lüge von diesem Wissen-Nichtwissen-Verhältnis weiß.[8] Daher teilt der Aufdecker einer Lüge mit der Lügnerin das Wissen, dass etwas anderes als die Lügenbehauptung zutrifft. Um eine Lüge aufzudecken, muss dieser Wissensbestand explizit gemacht werden. Im Unterschied zum Irrtum setzt Lügen eine Täuschungsabsicht voraus und kann der Lügnerin darum schuldhaft zugerechnet werden. Im Verschwörungsweltbild sind am Lügenvorwurf beteiligt: die Supermächtigen als schuldige Lügner, *Wir* als Belogene und Verschwörungsdenker als Aufdecker. Dabei reklamieren die Verschwörungsdenker genau genommen eine merkwürdige Doppelposition für sich: als Belogene und als Aufdecker. Das liegt daran, dass sich Verschwörungsdenker einerseits dem *Wir,* also der Gesamtheit der Belogenen, zurechnen, sich andererseits aber als »die Aufgewachten« davon ausnehmen (Vobruba 2024a: 62 ff.).

Tatsächlich beschäftigt sich die Verschwörungspublizistik intensiv damit, konkrete Gegenwahrheiten anzubieten. Es geht nicht anders, und zwar aus zwei Gründen. Wer den Vorwurf der Lüge nur taktisch verwendet, braucht doch Gegenwahrheiten, um ihn zu stabilisieren. Denn mit dem Vorwurf der Lüge wird der Anspruch glaubwürdiger Alternativen stets mit transportiert. Daran ändert sich auch nichts, wenn gar nicht deren Etablierung, sondern nur unspezifische Verunsicherung beabsichtigt ist. Denn angesichts etablierter Wahrheiten kann deren Verunsicherung nur über die Behauptung von Alternativwahrheiten führen (anders Kumkar 2022). In der Praxis dürfte unspezifische Verunsicherung ein nicht unerwünschter Nebeneffekt sein. Und wer verschwörungsdenkerische Wahrheiten ernsthaft vertritt, hat, wie wir soeben gesehen haben, ohnehin keine Wahl. So oder so gerät das Verschwörungsdenken in die Bredouille. Denn die modernen sozialen Verhältnisse sperren sich gegen einfache Erklärungen, das Verschwörungsdenken aber muss alles letztlich dem einen zentralen bösen Willen zu-

8 Obwohl eine Grundgegebenheit in sozialen Beziehungen, bringt die Soziologie, soweit ich sehe, für Lügen nur wenig Interesse auf. Eine Ausnahme ist der wenig bekannte Peter Stiegnitz (1936–2017), hauptberuflich ein hoher Beamter im österreichischen Bundeskanzleramt, der die Lügenwissenschaft, »Mentiologie«, als soziologische und psychologische Teildisziplin zu etablieren versuchte (vgl. Stiegnitz 1991).

ordnen. Darum wird aus dem Konzept der 15-Minuten-Stadt zur Verkehrsberuhigung in Metropolen ein »Freiluftgefängnis«, es werden aus Impfkampagnen Genozidversuche der Supermächtigen, aus der Agenda 21 der Vereinten Nationen ein Plan zur drastischen Bevölkerungsreduktion und aus der globalen Erwärmung eine neue Eiszeit, die demnächst bevorsteht. Solch Gegenwahrheiten zu verbreiten, ist mühsam.

4. Alles Lüge

Zum Glück ist die Behauptung, der Mainstream verbreite viele Lügen, im Verschwörungsweltbild inkonsequent. Denn folgt man seiner Logik, dann verbreitet der Mainstream nicht viele Lügen, sondern ausschließlich Lügen. Mit dem Beginn der Corona-Pandemie ist es passiert. Die Supermächtigen haben die Welt insgesamt »gefälscht«.[9] Ist man davon erst überzeugt, kann alles entlarvt werden, und die augenscheinliche Wirklichkeit wird zum Beweis für die Wahrheit ihres Gegenteils: Spricht der neue Chef der EU-Grenzschutzagentur Frontex die Einsicht aus, dass sich Grenzen nie völlig dicht machen lassen, wird im Verschwörungsweltbild daraus sein Geständnis, dass er seine Aufgabe darin sieht, »die völlige Abschaffung der europäischen Grenzen zu überwachen, während er vorgibt, sie zu sichern«.[10] Wirbt die WHO für gesunde Ernährung, lässt sich das »getrost als etwas ganz anderes erkennen, nämlich als Krieg gegen die Nahrungsmittelversorgung der Menschheit«.[11] Erklärt die WHO, man müsse für zukünftige Pandemien besser vorbereitet sein, beweist das, dass eine weitere Pandemie geplant ist. Dass die Eliten über Produktivitätsfortschritte durch künstliche Intelligenz diskutieren, beweist, dass sie massenhaft Beschäftigungslose schaffen und diese Überzähligen dann beseitigen wollen. Generell werden Ambivalenzen von Innovationen ins Katastrophische vereinseitigt und Warnungen vor prekären, regulierungsbedürftigen Entwicklungen (von KI etc.) zu deren vorbehaltloser Befürwortung umgedeutet. Im Rahmen des Verschwörungsweltbildes sind solche Schlussfolgerungen zwingend. Wie zwingend sie sind, lässt sich an der hohen Absurditätstoleranz erkennen, die diese Gegenwahrheiten erfordern.

---

9 Walter van Rossum, *Die Fälschung der Welt.* Manova 5.10.2023.

10 *Neuer Chef der EU-Grenzschutzagentur Frontex für offene Grenzen.* Uncut news 24.1.2024.

11 Thomas Fiedler, *Auf dem Teller ein Schrei.* Apolut 15.4.2024.

»Alles Lüge!« ist mehr als die Summe vieler einzelnen Lügen. Wird alles als Lüge angesehen, gerät die Wirklichkeit ins Rutschen. Denn die Behauptung impliziert einerseits, dass die Supermächtigen ein umfassend unzutreffendes Bild der Wirklichkeit entwerfen und verbreiten. Und sie geht andererseits über in die weitere Behauptung, dass die Supermächtigen die Wirklichkeit selbst entlang ihren Lügen gestalten. Das ist unrealistisch? Keineswegs! Es zeigt nur, wie mächtig sie sind. Der Überzeugung, dass alles Lüge ist, dass die Mächtigen die ganze Welt gefälscht haben, folgen fundamentale Zweifel auf dem Fuß, was wirklich Wirklichkeit ist. Die epistemische Verunsicherung nimmt zu, es drängen sich immer radikalere Fragen auf: »Was ist eigentlich real? Was ist wirklich geschehen? Und *ist* es überhaupt geschehen?«[12] Man kann auch sagen: Der Verschwörungsdiskurs wechselt von der Leitunterscheidung Lüge/Wahrheit zu Lüge/Wirklichkeit. Jetzt ist die Frage: »Wie sollen wir noch erkennen, was wirklich ist und was nicht?«[13]

5. Theater

Die grundlegende Verunsicherung des Verständnisses von Wirklichkeit im Verschwörungsweltbild kann man an der Vorliebe für Theatermetaphern ablesen. Darin zeigt sich auf den ersten Blick eine gewisse Nähe zur Soziologie. In die Soziologie wurde der Rollen-Begriff als Verbindung zwischen Strukturen und Handeln eingeführt. Dabei ging die Begriffsentwicklung vom »homo sociologicus«, der auf rollenkonformes Handeln festgelegt ist (Dahrendorf 2010), zum Verständnis von Rollen als Erwartungen (Plessner 1985: 229) und damit zugleich von »prinzipiell rollengemäß handelnden Menschen« zur empirisch offenen Konformitätsfrage (Popitz 1967: 41). Mit Hilfe des Rollenbegriffs kann Gesellschaft als ein Prozess anschaulich gemacht werden, in dem »wir alle« Theater spielen (Goffman 2021). Das ist keineswegs im Sinn der Aufdeckung von Unaufrichtigkeit gemeint, sondern soll begrifflich fassen, dass Handeln im Rahmen von Bündeln informeller und institutionell festgelegter Erwartungen stattfindet, die als Rollen bereit stehen. Man nimmt sie ein, geht in ihnen aber nicht auf. Sie können sich verändern und unter Umständen auch widersprüchlich sein, und die in ihnen

12 Tom Oliver Regenauer, *Der Vorhang fällt.* Manova 10.2.2024.
13 Charles Eisenstein, *Vorwärts in die Vergangenheit.* Manova 10.4.2024.

fixierten Erwartungen lassen sich erfüllen oder auch enttäuschen. Die Rollentheorie hatte anfangs einen starken Stabilitäts-Bias, da sie sich unter dem Eindruck der Frage nach der Vereinbarkeit individuellen Handelns mit dem Funktionieren der Gesellschaft entwickelte. Darum ging man erst von der strikten Bindung des Rollenträgers an seine Rolle aus und baute erst später Freiheitsgrade zwischen Rollen und ihren Trägerinnen ein.

Freiheitsgrade gibt es im verschwörungsdenkerischen Gesellschaftstheater nicht. Am deutlichsten wird das bei der gerne gebrauchten Metapher der Marionette. Die »Politikermarionette« hängt an Schnüren, die von den Mächtigen gezogen werden. Das Bild lässt keinen eigenen Handlungsspielraum zu. Jenseits dieser Extremvorstellung sollen Theatermetaphern die Manipulation anschaulich machen, der *wir* ausgesetzt sind. Da im Verschwörungsweltbild alles auf ein böses Handlungszentrum zurückgeführt wird, kann die Welt, so schlecht wie sie nun mal ist, nur aus Lügen bestehen. Diese Lügen kann man sich als eine Art Theaterstück vorstellen, das die Realität der bösen Absichten verbirgt. Vorne wird den Leuten ein Theater vorgespielt, bei dem die Supermächtigen Regie führen. Auf der Vorderbühne ist alles im Auftrag der Supermächtigen veranstaltete Lüge, zum Beispiel »das pandemische Theater«.[14]

> »Auf der Bühne wird ›Corona‹ gegeben – mit den bekannten Schauspielern Drosten, Lauterbach, Wieler, Söder, um nur vier der deutschen Akteure zu nennen. Als Bühnenbild: die Särge von Bergamo, die Intensivstation eines Krankenhauses mit Sauerstoff beatmete Patienten, Impfampullen, Impfbestecke – und nicht zu vergessen: die Darstellung des Virus, rot und mit nagelkopfartigen Tentakeln. Dann ist da aber auch noch die Hinterbühne – ganz wichtig! – der rückwärtig hinter dem Bühnenbild gelegene, für die Zuschauer nicht sichtbare Teil der Bühne. Dort ist das wahre Geschehen am Werk.«[15]

In diesem Beispiel: die Krisen des globalen Kapitalismus. Den Wenigen, die das Theater durchschauen, ist bekannt, dass Politik die Wirklichkeit verdeckt. Ein Text breitet es so aus: »Es wird nicht mehr gelogen, um eigene politische Ziele zu erreichen, die Lüge ist zum Selbstzweck der Politik geworden. Das heißt, Politik ist schlicht und einfach die soziale Artikulation der Lüge.«[16] Zur Plausibilisierung der Deckungsgleichheit von Lüge und Po-

---

14 Gerd Reuther, *Das pandemische Theater*. Manova 8.12.2023.

15 Rudolph Bauer, *Krisen, Pandemie und Großer Umbruch*. Hintergrund. Das Nachrichtenmagazin 13.10.2022.

16 Giorgio Agamben, *Theater und Politik*. tkp 15.2.2024.

litik müssen Volodymyr Selenski, Peppe Grillo und Ronald Reagan herhalten, also Personen die von Bühne und Film in die Politik gewechselt sind. Damit geht, so heißt es ohne weitere Begründung, eine Umkehrung einher. Wurde »früher und nicht nur im Theater – die Wahrheit durch das Zeigen und Entlarven der Unwahrheit erreicht [...], wird jetzt die Lüge durch das Zeigen und Entlarven der Wahrheit produziert«.[17] Die Gleichung ist schlicht: Schauspieler werden Politiker; Schauspiel wird zur Produktion von Lüge; voilà: Politik ist Lüge. Übergehen wir die Frage, ob es sich in all den drei Fällen um Schauspieler handelt. Der Autor meint, der Empirie auf der Spur zu sein, dokumentiert aber bloß Ahnungslosigkeit. Schauspiel ist keine Version von Lügen. Schon das Konzept von Schauspielerei als die »als ob«-Kunst (Konstantin S. Stanislawski) besagt das Gegenteil. Erst recht gilt das für das Konzept des epischen Theaters von Bertold Brecht und Caspar Neher (Tretow 2003), das eine anspruchsvolle Reflexionsleistung fordert: Von der Schauspielerin wird verlangt, etwas zu zeigen und zugleich »auch das Zeigen« zu zeigen. Das Bewusstsein des Publikums, im Theater zu sitzen, so als wären auch die »Zuschauer beim Theater beschäftigt« (Brecht 1973: 407, 412), ist für alle späteren Regiekonzepte konstitutiv, die im Kern auf ein Angebot (*nicht* Zwang) für das Publikum hinauslaufen, an der Aufführung aktiv teilzunehmen. Fluchtpunkt ist die gemeinsame Produktion der Wirklichkeit des Schauspiels. »Wir *alle* spielen Theater« gewinnt in einem solchen »Arbeitsbündnis« (Steinert 1998: 101) zwischen Schauspielern und Publikum einen eigenen Sinn.

Im soziologischen Verständnis wechseln die Leute die Positionen: Mal treten sie als Ensemble auf, mal sind sie Publikum, »dessen Interpretationstätigkeit für dieses Auftreten notwendig ist« (Goffman 2021: 231). Im Verschwörungsdenken dagegen steht die Arbeitsteilung fest. Die Schauspieler machen uns im Auftrag der Supermächtigen etwas vor, und *wir*, die große Mehrheit, lassen uns hinters Licht führen.

Also: Das Theater gründet nicht auf Lüge, genauso wenig wie die Soziologie Theatermetaphern verwendet, um Lügen aufzudecken.[18] Damit wird ein grundlegender Unterschied zwischen Soziologie und Verschwörungsdenken deutlich. Beide beziehen sich zwar auf Theater, aber in höchst unterschiedlicher Weise. In der Soziologie werden Theatermetaphern verwendet, um eine Grundgegebenheit des Prozessierens von Gesellschaft zu erfassen: Individuelles Handeln in Relation zu Gesellschaftlichkeit in Form von an die

17 Ebd.

18 Leider ist Goffman in diesem Punkt mehr als missverständlich (vgl. Goffman 2021: 65, 68).

Handelnden gerichteten Erwartungen. Die Verwendung von Theatermetaphern in der Soziologie hat den Sinn, theoretische Aussagen über die Wirklichkeit der Gesellschaft zu machen. Dagegen will das Verschwörungsdenken mit der Theatermetapher auf eine Scheinwirklichkeit hinweisen, die die wirkliche Wirklichkeit verbirgt. Die verschwörungsdenkerische Attitüde, hinter diesem Gesellschaftstheater eine authentische Wirklichkeit freizulegen, beruht auf der Vorstellung, es gebe hinter all den Erscheinungen »die absolute zeitlose Wirklichkeit«,[19] die epistemisch Halt bietet.

6. Vulgärkonstruktivismus

Was tun, wenn man meint, einer Welt ausgesetzt zu sein, in der böse Supermächtige die Fäden ziehen? Der Vorschlag zu einem harten Schnitt lautet: »Lassen Sie die Welt hinter sich!«[20] Aber das ist leichter gesagt, als getan. Immerhin hilft dabei eine Einstellung zur Realität, die Anleihen beim radikalen Konstruktivismus macht.

Eine Kernidee des radikalen Konstruktivismus, die von Teilen der Soziologie adaptiert wurde, lautet, dass wissenschaftlich nur das zugänglich sei, was Akteure als Welt konstruieren. So konstituiere sich Wirklichkeit, und mehr an harter Realität sei nicht zu haben. Für diese, hier natürlich unzulässig knapp charakterisierte, epistemologische Sicht ließe sich noch das folgende Argument ins Feld führen. Wenn es der Soziologie darum geht, herauszufinden, warum wie gehandelt wird, ist sie zwingend darauf angewiesen, jenes Bild der Wirklichkeit zu ermitteln, das das Handeln der Leute anleitet. Denn die Leute handeln nicht auf der Grundlage irgendeiner objektiven Realität, sondern orientiert daran, wie sie die Welt beobachten und interpretieren. Ein solches Argument für den radikalen Konstruktivismus wäre eine Art generalisiertes Thomastheorem. Ich weiß nicht, ob irgendjemand jemals so argumentiert hat. Hier dient es mir nur dazu, auf Grenzen des Konstruktivismus hinzuweisen. Das Argument besteht aus einer zutreffenden und einer nicht zutreffenden Komponente. Es trifft zu, dass Handeln danach ausgerichtet wird, wie Wirklichkeit von den Handelnden beobachtet und interpretiert wird. Aber es trifft nicht zu, dass dieses Interpretieren den beobachtenden Handelnden frei überlassen und in diesem Sinn beliebig ist. Ganz

---

19 Thomas Fiedler, *Auf dem Teller ein Schrei.* Apolut 15.4.2024.

20 Uncut news 12.1.2024.

im Gegenteil (Berger 2003: 220). Die Wirklichkeitsinterpretationen der Leute folgen harten Vorgaben der Realität. Selbstverständlich meldet sich die Realität nicht selbst zu Wort, aber sie teilt sich denen, für die sie *Lebens*realität ist, mit, indem auf durch inadäquate Interpretationen angeleitetes Handeln Schaden folgt. Der Realitätssinn der Leute erdet die Soziologie, indem sie deren Beobachtungen, Interpretationen und Handlungen, die alles andere als beliebig sind, beobachtet und interpretiert (Vobruba 2019: VII f.). Die Alltagsrealität konstituiert sich aus Rückkoppelungen zwischen Interpretationen und von ihnen angeleitetem Handeln unter der Rahmenbedingung, dass man aus seinem Handeln nicht andauernd Schaden erleiden will und kann. Die Außertäglichkeit der Sozialfigur des Helden, der für ein höheres Ideal bereit ist, dauerhaft Schaden zu erleiden, bestätigt dies. Darum lässt sich auch sagen: Der Ruf nach Heldentum ist eine Aufforderung zur Preisgabe des Realitätssinns. »Wir brauchen Helden und Heldentaten.«[21] Heldentum kann gute Gründe haben, es gibt aber kaum gute Gründe, andere dazu aufzurufen.

Das Verschwörungsdenken fühlt sich von der Idee, dass die Wirklichkeit ein Konstrukt ist, stark angezogen. »Die soziologische Theorie von der sozialen Konstruktion dürfte als bewiesen gelten.«[22] Radikal konstruktivistische Vorstellungen sind für das Verschwörungsdenken aus mehreren Gründen attraktiv. Erstens lassen sie sich zur Grundlage einer fundamentalen Wissenschaftsskepsis machen. Ian Hacking drückt das etwas derb, aber zutreffend, aus: »Richtig ist, daß sich viele Wissenschaftshasser und Nichtwisser an den Konstruktionismus anhängen, weil er ihre ohnmächtige Feindschaft gegen die Wissenschaft rechtfertige.« (Hacking 1999: 107) Aber die Attraktivität des radikalen Konstruktivismus für das Verschwörungsdenken geht darüber hinaus. Denn zweitens lässt sich die Wissenschaftsskepsis in Wirklichkeitsrelativismus überführen:

»Die erfundene Wirklichkeit, oder wie wirklich ist die Wirklichkeit, solche Bücher und Anleitung zum Unglücklichsein (alle drei Bücher von Paul Watzlawick) waren in den 1980er Jahren Bestseller. Der Konstruktivismus hatte Hochkonjunktur und es setzte sich in den Wissenschaften das Weltbild des Konstruktivismus durch. Namen wie Heinz von Foerster, Paul Watzlawick oder Niklas Luhmann und Ernst von Glasersfeld, kennen heute nur wenige.«[23]

21 Roland Rottenfußer, *Der Wind des Wandels*. Apolut 6.1.2024.
22 Anke Behrend, *Die kontrollierte Opposition*. Rubikon 9.12.2021.
23 Rüdiger Lenz, *Wahnsinn*. Apolut 22.12.2023.

Aber die Relativierung der Wirklichkeit allein reicht noch nicht. Die aus dem radikalen Konstruktivismus entlehnte Idee der rein subjektseitigen Wirklichkeitskonstruktion wird ins Verschwörungsweltbild integriert, indem die Clique der Supermächtigen als dominanter Konstrukteur eingeführt wird: »In unserer Zeit ist dieser Konstrukteur entlarvt. Weder Zufall noch Notwendigkeit beherrschen das gesellschaftliche und politische Geschehen. Seine Konstruktionen sind überdeutlich sichtbar.«[24] Also lässt sich drittens aus dem radikalen Konstruktivismus in verschwörungsdenkerischer Lesart ein Instrument im Kampf um die Wirklichkeit machen. Die Elite konstruiert, die anderen werden getäuscht und unterdrückt. »Die Plandemie war eine Konstruktion, der anthropogene Klimawandel ebenfalls.«[25] Dem will man etwas entgegenkonstruieren.

Die Idee, Wirklichkeit sei nichts als eine willkürliche Konstruktion, hat zwei Seiten. Einerseits lässt sie sich zu der Vorstellung passend machen, dass die Welt eine Fälschung der Supermächtigen ist. Andererseits aber kann man sie mit der Hoffnung verknüpfen, man könne alles auch ganz anders gestalten. Die Wahlverwandtschaft zwischen radikalem Konstruktivismus und Verschwörungsdenken verdankt sich einer einseitigen Wahl. Aber es lohnt, nach der Grundlage für diese Vorliebe zu fragen. Der radikale Konstruktivismus und das Verschwörungsweltbild haben gemeinsam, dass alles, was der Fall ist, im Kern handlungstheoretisch erklärt wird. Im Verschwörungsweltbild schaffen die Supermächtigen Wirklichkeit, in der Weltsicht des radikalen Konstruktivismus wird Wirklichkeit von denen erschaffen, die sie begrifflich fassen. Ohne Begriff keine Existenz seiner Sache. Bruno Latour hat das demonstriert. In mindestens zwei Anläufen kommt er zu dem Schluss, dass nicht stimmen kann, was französische Wissenschaftler in den 50er Jahren des 20. Jahrhunderts festgestellt haben: Ramses II kann nicht an Tuberkulose gestorben sein, weil der Tuberkulose-Bazillus erst im 19. Jahrhundert von Robert Koch entdeckt wurde (Latour 1998; Latour 2000). »Our brave scientists«, meint Latour etwas herablassend, könnten genauso behaupten, der Pharao sei mit einem Maschinengewehr getötet worden. Das hat es damals ja auch nicht gegeben. Der Kern des Arguments: Dem Bazillus kann keine echte Existenz zugebilligt werden, weil er noch nicht begrifflich gefasst war. Dass hier das Entdecken im Erfinden aufgeht, zeigt, dass auch die radikalkonstruktivistische Sicht der Welt handlungslogisch gestrickt ist. Darin findet sich das Verschwörungsdenken wieder. Viel spannender als die

24 Ebd.
25 Ebd.

Frage, warum diese Art der Wirklichkeitskonstruktion absurd ist, ist die Frage, welche Folgen ein solches Wirklichkeitsverständnis hat: Das radikalkonstruktivistische Verständnis der Wirklichkeit blockiert die Chance zu lernen.

»Das Erfahren hätte keine Chance, wäre die Welt, wie manche meinen, einfach das, was der Mensch in seinem unbegreiflichen schöpferischen Entwurf sie sein läßt. [...] Allein, so ist es nicht. Das, was wir Welt nennen, weist eine Eigenständigkeit auf, die sich beliebiger Interpretation widersetzt. Eben deshalb hat der Mensch überhaupt die Chance, zu lernen [...]« (Dux 1981: 495).

Die Auseinandersetzung mit dem radikalen Konstruktivismus aus schuldidaktischer Sicht[26] bestätigt diesen Einwand. Lernen und Lehren sind nur möglich, wenn die Subjekte ihre Umwelt als widerständige Wirklichkeit erfahren und sie somit nicht als vom Subjekt autonom konstruiert verstanden wird.

Nur in einer unangreifbaren Machtposition kann man es sich leisten, nicht zu lernen. Das ist die Rückwirkung[27] der von Macht eröffneten Chance, der Umwelt den eigenen Willen aufzuzwingen, auf die Machthaber. Man sieht: Radikaler Konstruktivismus und Machtphantasien konvergieren in eigenartiger Weise: Mit der Überzeugung, die Welt sei eine subjektseitige Konstruktion, begibt sich das Subjekt in die Position des Weltkonstrukteurs (von Foerster 2008). Mehr Machtphantasie geht nicht.

Klar, das Verschwörungsdenken ist viel schlichter angelegt als der radikale Konstruktivismus. Aber die Konsequenz ist dieselbe: Die Welt wird als ein Bau von Begriffen vorgestellt. So etwas lässt sich ungestraft denken, solange man mit der Wirklichkeit nichts vorhat. Das Verschwörungsdenken versteht sich aber als ein Denken mit praktischen Absichten und gerät so in die Sackgasse. Man verspricht sich von der konstruktivistischen Sicht auf die Welt eine Ermutigung zur großen Gesellschaftsveränderung. Unverkennbar übt die Idee subjektseitiger Beliebigkeit der Wirklichkeit starke Anziehungskraft auf das Verschwörungsdenken aus, weil es auf radikale Veränderung der sozialen Verhältnisse aus ist, aber ratlos vor der Machtfrage steht. Das einfache Kalkül lautet: Wenn alles Konstruktion ist, kann man auch alles anders konstruieren. »Die Achillesferse des Systems ist der Glaube einer

26 Vgl. dazu Oldenburg (2020) und die anschließende Diskussion zwischen Kollosche (2021) und Oldenburg (2021) in den Mitteilungen der Gesellschaft für Didaktik der Mathematik.

27 Die Soziologie hat sich, orientiert an Max Webers berühmter Definition von Macht (1972: 28), stark auf deren Wirkungen auf Machtunterworfene konzentriert (vgl. etwa Lukes 1974) und Rückwirkungen von Macht auf Machthaber weitgehend ausgespart.

Mehrheit an seine Legitimation. Es hat nur so viel Macht, wie wir ihm zugestehen.«[28] Doch mit der Zweckentfremdung des radikalen Konstruktivismus als Instrument gesellschaftlicher Totalveränderung kehrt die Machtfrage durch die Hintertür zurück: Die Supermächtigen konstruieren die Welt. Sie ließe sich auch anders konstruieren. So entsteht der Mehrwert des Vulgärkonstruktivismus. *Wir* würden sie anders konstruieren, aber *uns* fehlt die Macht dazu. Der Mehrwert verflüchtigt sich wieder.

An dieser Stelle zeichnet sich die fundamentale Differenz zwischen Soziologie und Verschwörungsdenken ab. Der Konstruktivismus hat die Rolle des Beobachters/der Beobachterin in einer Weise radikalisiert, die das Verschwörungsdenken, so sehr es sich auch angezogen fühlt, nicht mitmachen kann. Nachdem Comte die Beobachtung der Einbildungskraft vorgeordnet hatte, war die Präzisierung der Rolle der Beobachterin/des Beobachters der nächste entscheidende Schritt zur Realisierung des empirischen Zugriffs der Soziologie auf das, was gesellschaftlich der Fall ist: ihr Rückzug von einer zentralen Beobachtungsposition zur Beobachtung zweiter Ordnung. Alfred Schütz hat das prägnant formuliert: »Jeder, der Sozialwissenschaftler werden will, muss sich entschließen, einen anderen statt seiner selbst als das Zentrum dieser Welt zu setzen, nämlich die beobachtete Person.« (Schütz 1972: 41) Dadurch eröffnen sich zwei Chancen: Zum einen findet die Soziologie Anschluss an den Realitätssinn der Leute, und zum anderen kann sie sich selbst zum Objekt der Beobachtung zweiter Ordnung machen und so in einer Reflexionsschleife ihre eigenen Interpretationen zu ihrem Thema machen. Beide Möglichkeiten verstellt sich das Verschwörungsdenken durch die Ableitung seiner Interpretationen aus dem absoluten Anfang: Interpretationen der Leute sind ihm nicht Datum, sondern nur das Ergebnis von Täuschung durch die Supermächtigen. Und die Verbindlichkeit der eigenen Position, die den Leuten entgegengehalten wird, steht durch die Unhinterfragbarkeit des absoluten Anfangs immer schon fest.[29] Was aber widerfährt dem Verschwörungsweltbild, wenn es von der Relativierung der Realität, die es betreibt, selbst erfasst wird? Da die Stabilität und Erklärungskraft des Verschwörungsweltbildes auf der Unbefragbarkeit seines absoluten Ausgangspunktes beruht, muss dessen Erschütterung eine Dynamik in Gang setzen, die weltbildintern nicht beherrschbar ist.

Der Vulgärkonstruktivismus ist der entscheidende Schritt des Verschwörungsdenkens raus aus der Wirklichkeit. Kurz noch einmal der Weg dahin:

28 Tom-Oliver Regenauer, *Der Vorhang fällt*. Manova 10.2.2024.

29 Dirk Baecker hat mich auf diese Konsequenz aufmerksam gemacht. Danke.

Erst zahlreiche Lügen; dann die Überzeugung, dass alles gefälscht ist, samt der Umkehrung von Lüge und Wahrheit. Und schließlich die Generalisierung des Zweifels am Realitätsgehalt der Wirklichkeit. Dieser Zweifel muss schließlich zu dem Verdacht führen, man selbst sei Teil der üblen Totalität und von den Supermächtigen in deren Plan eingebaut.

7. Selbstverdacht und Ausbruchsversuche

Das Verschwörungsweltbild erfasst und kritisiert Gesellschaft als »Totalität«. »Wenn das Ganze das Falsche ist, dann müssen wir das Ganze ins Visier nehmen.«[30] Damit gerät die verschwörungsdenkerische Gesellschaftskritik in jenen performativen Widerspruch (ausführlich Vobruba 2024a: 120 ff.), der auch einigen Ansätzen sozialwissenschaftlicher Gesellschaftskritik nicht fremd ist: Wie lassen sich totale gesellschaftliche Vereinnahmung, durch Macht oder durch Manipulation, und die herrschaftliche Inpflichtnahme individuellen Eigensinns kritisieren, wenn man doch selbst der Totalität angehört? Konsequent erwägen manche Verschwörungstexte den Verdacht: »Das Gerücht, dass Eliten uns beherrschen, haben diese wahrscheinlich selbst in die Welt gesetzt.«[31] Wenn die Gesellschaft insgesamt eine Inszenierung der Supermächtigen ist, wie soll man sie dann erkennen? Konkreter: Wie geht man mit dem Selbstverdacht um, dass der eigene Widerstand Teil des lügenhaften Theaters ist? Reaktion darauf ist entweder Ratlosigkeit oder ein souveräner Bruch mit der Logik: Die Manipulation durch die Supermächtigen erfasst ja doch nicht alle, sondern nur die große Mehrheit, die »Schlafschafe«. Das ist zwar inkonsistent, hat aber den Vorteil, dass man den performativen Widerspruch abschüttelt und sich zugleich in eine schmeichelhafte Durchblicker-Position bringt. Allerdings hat man damit nicht nur die Supermächtigen, sondern auch die Mehrheit gegen sich. Das kann man zwar erklären; sei es, indem man den Mainstream-Medien unbeschränkte Manipulationsmacht zuschreibt, sei es, indem man »Massenhalluzinationsprozesse«[32] diagnostiziert. Aber all das ändert nichts an dem Problem der Verschwörungsdenker, dass sie rettungslos in der Minderheit sind.

30 Walter van Rossum, *Die Fälschung der Welt*. Manova 5.10.2023.
31 Karsten Ramser, *Hoffnungslos optimistisch*. Rubikon 10.8.2022.
32 Kai-Uwe Herthneck, *Die Gewissenlosen*. Manova 14.2.2024.

Zwar gibt es von Zeit zu Zeit Versuche, aus der Isolation auszubrechen, indem man publizistisch Themen und praktisch Demonstrationen zu kapern versucht. Auffällig war dies im Zuge der Bauerndemos gegen die Streichung der Subvention des Agrardiesels im Januar 2024. Das ging so weit, dass die Sympathiebekundung mit den Anliegen der Bauern mit der Forderung verknüpft wurde, es sei »eine Fundamentalkritik der Naturwissenschaften als gedanklicher Rahmen der Moderne – auch bezogen auf die landwirtschaftlichen Entwicklungen – unumgänglich«.[33] Aber die Hoffnungen, der Bauernprotest werde die Moderne aus den Angeln heben oder zumindest »der Beginn einer weitaus größeren Protestbewegung sein, bis hin zum Generalstreik und zu einem grundlegenden Politikwechsel«,[34] waren vergebens. Die Avancen der »Schwachköpfe mit Umsturzphantasien«, der »Radikalen« und »Spinner« (© Deutscher Bauernverband)[35] stießen auf wenig Gegenliebe. Dafür wiederum konnte man die Bauernverbände verantwortlich machen, die angeblich die wahren Interessen der Bauern verrieten. Aber das änderte nichts: Die Bauernproteste boten keinen Ausweg aus der verschwörungsdenkerischen Einsamkeit.

8. Losing my Religion

Karl Popper hat in der »Konspirationstheorie der Gesellschaft«, wie er das Verschwörungsweltbild nannte, »ein typisches Resultat der Säkularisierung religiösen Aberglaubens« gesehen (Popper 1972: 119). Tatsächlich vermittelt die logische Struktur eine gewisse Verwandtschaft. Vor diesem Hintergrund hat Popper Verschwörungsdenken als ein Übergangsphänomen aufgefasst, das mit der sich durchsetzenden Säkularisierung verschwindet. Das könnte so sein und führt schließlich zu der umfassendsten Generalisierung des im Verschwörungsweltbild angelegten Wirklichkeitszweifels: Zweifel an der Wirklichkeit der Verschwörung. Gibt es denn die Steuerung der Welt durch die Mächtigen wirklich? Das Verschwörungsweltbild generiert Zweifel an der Wirklichkeit in einer solchen Radikalität, dass er sich gegen das Verschwörungsweltbild selbst richtet. Wenn die Wirklichkeit gefälscht und eine

33 Uli Fischer, *Der Bauern-Aufstand.* Manova 11.1.2024.

34 Milosz Matouschek, *Die Power der Bauern.* Manova 9.1.2024.

35 Empört zitiert von Dr. Peter F. Mayer, *Deutscher Bauernverband beschimpft unerwünschte Teilnehmer an geplanter Kundgebung rüde.* tkp 28.12.2023.

Konstruktion in einem denkbar üblen Sinn des Wortes ist, ist dann die Verschwörung der Eliten gegen uns *wirklich*? Anhand der Geschichte *Alice in Wonderland* von Lewis Carroll erwägt eine Autorin, ob bei der Frage »Wer steckt dahinter?«, überhaupt etwas rauskommt.

»You dive down rabbit hole after rabbit hole, searching for the man behind the curtain. [...] You dig even deeper. You discover that you haven't just been fed false information about how governments and nations work, you've been fed false information about even your most basic assumptions about reality. [...] But in all this rabbit holing and discovering, you still don't find any man behind the curtain. [...] And you realize then that there is no man behind the curtain, and there never was. [...] And you're not even mad. In fact, you find it hilarious. You laugh and you laugh at the silliness of it all.«[36]

Das ist die Preisgabe jeglicher Orientierung. Ob daraus ein Gewaltausbruch (Vobruba 2024a: 112 ff.) oder permanente Resignation folgt, ist nur noch Geschmackssache.

Ich fasse zusammen. Die Relativierung der Wirklichkeit richtet sich erst gegen den Mainstream. Das erzeugt Folgeprobleme, die wieder im Rahmen des Weltbildes bearbeitet werden müssen, womit sich die zunehmende Relativierung verselbständigt. Der generalisierte Zweifel führt schließlich an jenen Punkt, an dem das Verschwörungsdenken nicht mehr in der Lage ist, seiner eigenen Wirklichkeit zu trauen. Das ist keine Befreiung, es ist ein Totalverlust.

9. Spuren

Soziologie und Verschwörungsdenken haben den Anspruch gemeinsam, Gesellschaft insgesamt zu erfassen. Für die Soziologie manifestiert sich dies etwa im Anspruch auf Zuständigkeit für die »gesellschaftliche Totalität« (Adorno 1972: 81) oder im Desiderat einer »Theorie, die alles Soziale einschließt und alles andere ausschließt« (Luhmann 2005: 259). Das Verschwörungsdenken fasst Gesellschaft insgesamt in den Blick, indem es sie von einem bösen Handlungszentrum aus interpretiert, das die sozialen Verhältnisse völlig im Griff hat. Um es zu wiederholen: »Wenn das Ganze das

36 Caitlin Johnston, *Rabbit Holes, Men behind Curtains.* LAProgressive 13.9.2023.

Falsche ist, dann müssen wir das Ganze ins Visier nehmen.«[37] Der umfassende Zugriff der Supermächtigen auf die Gesellschaft erfordert, sie als Ganze zu kritisieren und fundamental neu aufzustellen.

Das Spezifische des Zugangs der Soziologie zu Gesellschaft bestand von ihren Anfängen an darin, dass sie ihren Gegenstand der traditional-absolutistischen Logik zu entwinden trachtete, sich also bemühte, ihn nachmetaphysisch zu fassen. Die Soziologie, schreibt Siegfried Krakauer, entwickelte sich aus der nicht mehr vom Sinn durchdrungenen Welt. Das »Subjekt, das vorher einbezogen war in den Reigen der die Welt erfüllenden Gestalten, entsteigt nun vereinsamt dem Chaos als alleiniger Träger des Geistes, und vor seinem Blick öffnen sich die unermesslichen Reiche der Realität.« (Krakauer 1971: 13) Es kann hier dahingestellt bleiben, ob dies der Theorie der Gesellschaft dadurch gelungen ist, dass »sie die Gesellschaft als jenes Substrat bestimmt, das der traditionellen Philosophie ewige Wesenheiten hieß oder Geist« (Adorno 1972: 81). Hier geht es um den Nachweis des Anspruchs, nicht um seine Einlösung. Jedenfalls bedeutet die Auflösung des traditional-absolutistischen Weltbildes, der sich die Soziologie verdankt, den Verlust von endgültigen Antworten durch den Rückgriff auf einen absoluten Anfang; und zugleich die Befreiung ihrer Perspektive auf immer weiter reichende, dichtere Zusammenhänge und daran anschließende immer neue Fragen.

Dem Verschwörungsdenken ist dieser Prozess nur Verlust. »Die abendländische Naturwissenschaft und rationale Philosophie postulierte dann ›Natur‹ als bloße Außenwelt ohne ein Innen, als die Bühne unseres Seins. […] Der Nihilismus trat seinen Siegeszug an, der bis heute andauert.«[38] Hoffnungen richten sich auf »die Wirkmächte jenseits der materiellen Welt, die sich dem Willen des Weltenschöpfers verpflichtet fühlen und permanent auf die Verhältnisse mit einwirken.«[39] Dazu braucht es – folgerichtig – »die allgemeine echte Resakralisierung des Lebens«.[40] Soziologie und Verschwörungsdenken entwickelten sich beide im Umbruch der Weltbilder. Sie reagieren darauf aber höchst unterschiedlich. Die Entwicklung der Soziologie lässt sich als Geschichte der Bemühungen lesen, die traditionalen Reste von (Welt-)Erklärung loszuwerden. Das Verschwörungsdenken dagegen versucht, den modernen sozialen Verhältnissen traditional-absolutistisches Erklären überzustülpen.

---

37 Walter van Rossum, *Die Fälschung der Welt.* Manova 5.10.2023.

38 Jochen Kirchhoff, *Die Welt ohne uns.* Manova 17.8.2023.

39 Uli Fischer, *Wohin die Reise geht.* Manova 3.11.2023.

40 Uli Fischer, *Dichtung und Wahrheit.* Manova 20.1.2024.

Entlang der Darstellung des schrittweisen Verlustes der Wirklichkeit, den das Verschwörungsdenken erfährt, haben sich soziologische Spuren gefunden. Soziologie und Verschwörungsdenken stellen Behauptungen über Zusammenhänge in der Gesellschaft auf. Aber die Soziologie nimmt die beobachtete Wirklichkeit, um ihre Behauptungen zu überprüfen. Das Verschwörungsdenken dagegen immunisiert ihre Behauptungen mit dem Lügenvorwurf. Das soziologische Rollenkonzept weist mit dem Verschwörungsweltbild eine Schnittmenge auf, wenn Rollen deterministisch verstanden werden. Eine deutliche Affinität des Verschwörungsdenkens zum radikalen Konstruktivismus ergibt sich daraus, dass er Machbarkeitsillusionen vermittelt und Erfahrung neutralisiert.

Die Differenz zwischen der Soziologie und dem Verschwörungsdenken ist im Kern die Differenz zwischen dem Denken auf moderner Grundlage und einem Denken, das sich gegen die Moderne richtet. Das Verschwörungsweltbild erklärt alles, was der Fall ist, durch den Verweis auf ein mächtiges Handlungszentrum. Soziologisches Erklären ist relational und führt genau *nicht* zu einem absoluten Ausgangspunkt zurück. Als soziologische Spuren im Verschwörungsdenken erscheinen traditionale Denkreste der Soziologie, da diese ins Verschwörungsweltbild passen. Wer will, kann das Verschwörungsdenken als einen Lackmustest für die Soziologie verwenden: Soziologische Spuren im Verschwörungsdenken sprechen für einen unaufgeklärten Rest traditionalen Denkens in der Soziologie, das zu überwinden sie historisch angetreten ist.

Literatur

Adorno, Theodor W. 1972: Soziologie und empirische Forschung. In Theodor W. Adorno / Hans Albert / Ralf Dahrendorf / Jürgen Habermas / Harald Pilot / Karl R. Popper, Der Positivismusstreit in der deutschen Soziologie. Darmstadt, Neuwied: Luchterhand, 81–101.

Berger, Johannes 2003: Neuerliche Anfragen an die Theorie der funktionalen Differenzierung. In Hans-Joachim Giegel / Uwe Schimank (Hg.), Beobachter der Moderne. Frankfurt am Main: Suhrkamp, 207–230.

Boltanski, Luc 2013: Rätsel und Komplotte: Kriminalliteratur, Paranoia, moderne Gesellschaft. Berlin: Suhrkamp.

Brecht, Bertolt 1973: Über den Beruf des Schauspielers. In Bertolt Brecht, Gesammelte Werke 15. Schriften zum Theater I. Frankfurt am Main: Suhrkamp, 389–436.

Comte, Auguste 1933 [1824]: Die Soziologie. Die positive Philosophie im Auszug. Hgg. von Friedrich Blaschke. Leipzig: Alfred Kröner.

Dahrendorf, Ralf 2010 [1959]. Homo Sociologicus. 17. Auflage. Wiesbaden: Springer VS.

Dux, Günter 1981: Anfang und Richtungssinn der Geschichte. Die soziologische Dimension der Ontogenese für ihr Verständnis. Merkur Nr. 396, 488–496.

Dux, Günter 2017 [2000]: Historisch-genetische Theorie der Kultur. 4. Auflage. Gesammelte Schriften Band 2. Wiesbaden: Springer VS.

Goffman, Erving 2021 [1959]: Wir alle spielen Theater. Die Selbstdarstellung im Alltag. 19. Auflage. München: Piper.

Hacking, Ian 1999: Was heißt ›soziale Konstruktion‹? Zur Konjunktur einer Kampfvokabel in den Wissenschaften. Frankfurt am Main: Fischer.

James, Harold 2022: Schockmomente. Eine Weltgeschichte von Inflation und Globalisierung 1850 bis heute. Freiburg im Breisgau: Herder.

Kästner, Erich 1932: Die Sache mit den Klößen. In Erich Kästner, Das verhexte Telefon (Illustrationen von Walter Trier). Berlin-Grunewald: Williams & Co.

Kollosche, David 2021: Abarbeiten am Konstruktivismus – Bemerkungen zum Beitrag von Reinhard Oldenburg in den Mitteilungen der GDM 109. Mitteilungen der Gesellschaft für Didaktik der Mathematik 110, 77–84.

Krakauer, Siegfried 1971: Soziologie als Wissenschaft. In Siegfried Krakauer, Schriften I. Frankfurt am Main: Suhrkamp, 9–101.

Kumkar, Nils 2022: Alternative Fakten. Zur Praxis der kommunikativen Erkenntnisverweigerung. Berlin: Suhrkamp.

Latour, Bruno 1998: Ramsès II est-il mort de la tuberculose? La Recherche 307, 84–85.

Latour, Bruno 2000: On the partial existence of existing and nonexisting objects. In Lorraine Daston (ed.), Biographies of scientific objects. Chicago, IL: University of Chicago Press, 247–269.

Luhmann, Niklas 2005: Einführung in die Theorie der Gesellschaft. Hgg. von Dirk Baecker. Heidelberg: Carl Auer.

Lukes, Steven 1974: Power. A Radical View. Houndmills, Basingstoke: Macmillan Press.

Oldenburg, Reinhard 2020: Realistischer Konstruktivismus. Ein unwissenschaftlicher Beitrag. Mitteilungen der Gesellschaft für Didaktik der Mathematik 109, 77–84.

Oldenburg, Reinhard 2021: Konstruktivismus abgearbeitet. Eine Antwort auf David Kollosche: Abarbeiten am Konstruktivismus in den Mitteilungen der GDM 110. Mitteilungen der Gesellschaft für Didaktik der Mathematik 111, 63–64.

Plessner, Helmuth 1985 [1960]: Soziale Rolle und menschliche Natur. In Helmuth Plessner, Schriften zur Soziologie und Sozialphilosophie. Gesammelte Schriften X. Frankfurt am Main: Suhrkamp, 227–240.

Popitz, Heinrich 1967: Der Begriff der Rolle als Element der soziologischen Theorie. Tübingen: J.C.B. Mohr.

Popper, Karl 1972 [1949]: Prognose und Prophetie in den Sozialwissenschaften. In Ernst Topitsch (Hg.), Logik der Sozialwissenschaften. Köln: Kiepenheuer & Witsch, 113–125.

Schimank, Uwe 2015: Modernity as a functionally differentiated capitalist society. A general theoretical model. European Journal of Social Theory, vol. 18, no. 4, 413–430.

Schütz, Alfred 1972 [1940]: Das Problem der Rationalität in der sozialen Welt. In Alfred Schütz, Gesammelte Aufsätze II. Studien zur soziologischen Theorie. Hgg. von Arvid Brodersen. Den Haag: Martinus Nijhoff, 22–50.

Simmel, Georg 1992 [1908]: Soziologie. Untersuchungen über die Formen der Vergesellschaftung. Frankfurt am Main: Suhrkamp.

Steinert, Heinz 1998: Kulturindustrie. Münster: Westfälisches Dampfboot.

Stiegnitz, Peter 1991: Lügen lohnt sich. Lüge-Wahrheit-Wirklichkeit. Frankfurt am Main: Haag und Herchen.

Tretow, Christine 2003: Caspar Neher – Graue Eminenz hinter der Brecht-Gardine und den Kulissen des modernen Musiktheaters. Eine Werkbiographie. Trier: Wissenschaftlicher Verlag Trier.

Vobruba, Georg 2019: Die Gesellschaft der Leute. Kritik und Gestaltung der sozialen Verhältnisse. 2. Auflage. Wiesbaden: Springer VS.

Vobruba, Georg 2024a: Das Verschwörungsweltbild. Denken gegen die Moderne. Weinheim, Basel: Beltz Juventa.

Vobruba, Georg 2024b: Logik und Leistungsfähigkeit des Verschwörungsweltbildes. Berliner Journal für Soziologie. Band 34, Heft 1, 77–102.

von Foerster, Heinz 2008: Der Anfang von Himmel und Erde hat keinen Namen. Eine Selbsterschaffung in sieben Tagen. Berlin: Kadmos.

Wagner, Gerhard 2001: Auguste Comte zur Einführung. Hamburg: Junius.

Weber, Max 1972 [1921/1922]: Wirtschaft und Gesellschaft. Tübingen: J.C.B. Mohr.

SOZIOLOGIE, 53. JG., HEFT 3, 2024, S. 305–319

Dekolonisierung als Dekanonisierung?

Zur Ortsbestimmung Lateinamerikas und der Karibik in der soziologischen Wissensproduktion und -rezeption

Anika Oettler, Clara Ruvituso, Fabio Santos

In der SOZIOLOGIE wurde jüngst das hausgemachte Problem fehlender Expertise zu Osteuropa diskutiert (Worschech et al. 2023) und für eine »Soziologie der Weltgesellschaft« (Schlichte 2023) plädiert: eine Soziologie, die ihr Personal, ihren Kanon und ihre Fragestellungen global ausrichtet und sich nicht bloß auf eine methodologisch fragwürdige Fokussierung einer Handvoll Länder Nordwesteuropas und Nordamerikas beschränkt (siehe auch Bogusz 2018; Koloma Beck 2018). Diesen Diagnosen und Forderungen schließen wir uns uneingeschränkt an, möchten die Diskussion jedoch regional, theoretisch und soziologiegeschichtlich erweitern, indem wir das reichhaltige Archiv soziologischer Forschung aus und über Lateinamerika und die Karibik durchforsten.[1]

Diese Erweiterung der Debatte durch Rückbindung an deutlich frühere Debatten fußt darauf, dass die Anerkennung der Bewahrungswürdigkeit des in anderen geographischen Kontexten produzierten soziologischen Wissens

1 Dem vorliegenden Beitrag liegen Diskussionen zugrunde, die auf Grundlage des Vortrags von Anika Oettler sowie der Buchankündigung von Clara Ruvituso und Fabio Santos auf der vergangenen Herbsttagung der DGS-Sektion Soziologiegeschichte an der Goethe-Universität Frankfurt am Main entstanden sind. Die Tagung »Diversifizierung – Dezentrierung – Dekolonisierung. Zur (Un-)Sichtbarmachung der Soziologiegeschichte« wurde von Takemitsu Morikawa, Doris Schweitzer und Fabio Santos organisiert. Wir bedanken uns ausdrücklich bei allen Beteiligten.

noch viel weiter gehen könnte, wenn sie von der Vorstellung Abschied nähme, dass für die Soziologiegeschichtsschreibung die Ausschnitte oder Gesamtwerke einzelner Personen ausschlaggebend sind. Was für die bildende Kunst gilt, wenden wir auch auf die Soziologie an: Ihr Kanon ist »both a discursive structure and a structure of masculine narcissism within the exercise of cultural hegemony« (Pollock 1999: xiv[2]).

Die begrüßenswerte Erweiterung des soziologischen Kanons um Autor:innen jenseits Nordwesteuropas und Nordamerikas oder um marginalisierte Autor:innen wie beispielsweise W.E.B. Du Bois innerhalb dieser unhinterfragten Zentren läuft Gefahr, in dreifacher Hinsicht neue Ausschlüsse zu produzieren: Erstens werden nur jene Autor:innen gehört, die an die aktuellen post- und dekolonialen Debatten in den Zentren anschlussfähig sind. Mit einer solchen, auf hiesige Belange ausgerichteten selektiven Lesart werden zweitens oftmals diejenigen Teile in den Werken dieser Autor:innen ausgeblendet, die historisch-materialistische Zeitdiagnosen oder marxistische Argumentationen liefern. Drittens wird bei diesen Debatten außer Acht gelassen, dass es auch im deutschsprachigen Raum eine Tradition der Soziologie Lateinamerikas (in geringerem Maße auch der Karibik) gegeben hat, die sich in unterschiedliche Stränge auffächert und von Analysen revolutionärer Entwicklungen (unter anderem Meschkat 2010) und dependenztheoretischen Debatten (unter anderem Senghaas 1974) bis hin zu landeskundlichen Einführungen (unter anderem Sandner, Steger 1973) und »bindestrichsoziologischen« Beiträgen zu Geschlechterverhältnissen, zivilgesellschaftlichen Entwicklungen und Umweltdiskursen reicht (unter anderem Braig, Ferdinand, Zapata 1997).

Um unser Argument zu entfalten, skizzieren wir erstens die mit der Ausweitung des Kanons oftmals verbundene Verkürzung am Beispiel der späten, gegenwärtig regen Rezeption Aníbal Quijanos, zweitens die (vergessene) produktive Rezeption der *Dependencia*-Ansätze in den 1970er und 1980er Jahren und drittens die Entwicklung der deutschen Lateinamerikaforschung. Mit dieser fachgeschichtlichen Rekonstruktion und Re-Lektüre argumentieren wir, dass die gegenwärtige Beschränkung der hiesigen Soziologie auf nordwesteuropäische und nordamerikanische Kontexte historisch keine Konstante darstellt und deshalb mit Blick auf die Zukunft durchaus wandelbar ist. Dieser positive Befund hin zu der von Schlichte postulierten »Soziologie der Weltgesellschaft« oder einer »Globalen Soziologie« (Santos, Ruvituso 2024) erfordert jedoch eine Reihe struktureller Veränderungen, von

2 Siehe für die Soziologie auch Curato (2013: 272).

denen wir die Öffnung des Kanons und die produktive Hinterfragung der Trennung von Soziologie und Regionalwissenschaften als besonders wichtig erachten. Werden diese angegangen, erübrigen sich auch hitzige Debatten über die Neuentdeckung und Relevanz post- und dekolonialer Ansätze, wie sie im Nachgang des wichtiges Anstoßes von Manuela Boatcă, Sina Farzin und Julian Go (2018) auch in der SOZIOLOGIE geführt wurden.

Ausweitungen, Verkürzungen und Wissenshierarchien

In ihrem UNESCO-Bericht »Where are social sciences produced?« haben die Soziologen Yves Gingras und Sébastien Mosbah-Natanson 2010 gezeigt, dass die weltweite Produktion sozialwissenschaftlichen Wissens eine zutiefst ungleiche Struktur aufweist: Betrachtet man die von Thomson-Web-of-Science-Datenbanken indexierten Zeitschriften, so zeigt sich eine enorme Konzentration der Produktion in den Zentren des globalen Nordens (USA und Teile Europas) und eine wachsende Hegemonie des Englischen. Lateinamerika und Afrika sind in diesem Mainstream-Circuit kaum vertreten. Lenken wir den Blick jedoch auf andere Datenbanken wie die lateinamerikanischen SciELO, Redalyc und Latindex, so erkennen wir eine rege sozialwissenschaftliche Produktion in spanischer und portugiesischer Sprache, die parallel zu den Mainstream-indexierten Systemen läuft und in nationale und/oder regionale Systeme von mehrheitlich Open Access Zeitschriften und lokal veröffentlichten Büchern eingebunden ist (Beigel et al. 2024a, 2024b). Dieses Wissen wird trotz des pionierhaften freien Zugangs kaum in den Zentren rezipiert. Als Reaktion auf die exkludierenden Publikationsmechanismen und Anerkennungslogiken der nordamerikanischen und europäischen Wissenschaft haben sich in Lateinamerika und der Karibik heterogene Produktionsräume mit eigenen regionalen Zentren und Kreisläufen herausgebildet. Die Soziologin Maristella Svampa argumentiert, dass Lateinamerika unter einem »Akkumulationsdefizit« ihrer theoretischen Wissensproduktion leidet. Als Gründe für dieses Defizit nennt Svampa neben den historischen Unterbrechungen akademischer Laufbahnen durch Diktaturen, Exil und politische Verfolgung auch strukturelle, institutionelle und finanzielle Engpässe sowie intellektuelle Abhängigkeiten und den internen Kolonialismus (Svampa 2016).

Dass Lateinamerika und die Karibik weiterhin eine Leerstelle im soziologischen Kanon bilden (Ausnahmen bestätigen die Regel), scheint uns ein

Zeichen dafür zu sein, dass den durchaus regen Diskussionen über die Dekolonisierung unserer Wissensbestände eine anglophone beziehungsweise an der britischen Kolonialgeschichte orientierte Schlagseite zugrunde liegt. Dies wiederum ist ein Indiz für eine Hierarchie innerhalb der Zentren (in diesem Fall Europas), in denen das britische Wissenschaftssystem und englischsprachige Publikationen eine deutlich höhere Sichtbarkeit erlangen als andere Länder und Sprachen. Diese neue Kanonbildung postkolonial informierter Soziologie hat sich in konzentrischen Kreisen um die Theorien Edward W. Saids, Gayatri Chakravorty Spivaks und Homi K. Bhabhas entwickelt (do Mar Castro Varela, Dhawan 2015). Eine solch einseitige Verortung postkolonialer Perspektiven im anglophonen Raum sowie darüber hinaus in der kultur- oder literaturwissenschaftlichen Diskussion und im nachkolonialen Kontext schmälert den Ruf und die Relevanz postkolonialer Forschung für die und innerhalb der Soziologie (Boatcă, Costa 2010: 73). Die jüngste Erweiterung um dekoloniale Perspektiven aus der Feder lateinamerikanischer Autor:innen, die zwischenzeitlich oder langfristig an US-amerikanischen Eliteeinrichtungen beheimatet waren oder sind, bringt eigene Ausschlüsse mit sich, wie die bolivianische Soziologin Silvia Rivera Cusicanqui beobachtet: Es entstehe ein neuer selbstreferenzieller Kanon mit neuen »Gurus«, die mit kulturellem und sozialem Kapital ausgestattet sind, das ihnen Gastprofessuren, Keynotes und einen Platz in der Bibliographie dekolonialer Forschung sichere (Rivera Cusicanqui 2020: 297).

Dass sich hier ein »racialized and exoticised multiculturalism in the academies« (ebd.) zu etablieren beginnt, wird durch die verkürzte und auf hiesige Debatten zugeschnittene Rezeption lateinamerikanischer Autor:innen noch verstärkt. Das Œuvre von Aníbal Quijano ist ein hervorragendes Beispiel, denn es handelt sich hier um weit mehr als eine dekoloniale Theorie, die die westliche Moderne hinterfragt. Der 1967 gegründete Dachverband von lateinamerikanischen sozialwissenschaftlichen Forschungseinrichtungen CLACSO mit Sitz in Buenos Aires hat 2020 eine 958-seitige *Antología Esencial* – eine Zusammenstellung der wichtigsten Werke Quijanos – herausgegeben. Hier zeigt sich sehr deutlich, welchen Weg sein Versuch genommen hat, die peruanische, lateinamerikanische und globale Wirklichkeit zu verstehen. Wie viele lateinamerikanische Intellektuelle seiner Zeit hatte er sich zunächst mit den Arbeiten von Marx und Trotzki befasst und sich mit diesem Rüstzeug mit der gesellschaftlichen Wirklichkeit Perus auseinandergesetzt. Es ging ihm in den 1960er Jahren um ein Verständnis der bäuerlichen Bewegungen und der indigenen Frage, um Abhängigkeitsstrukturen,

Urbanisierungs- und Marginalisierungsprozesse. In den 1970er Jahren interessierte er sich vor allem für die Kernfragen der Revolution in Lateinamerika (Anti-Imperialismus oder Arbeiter:innenkampf) und das progressive Militärregime unter Juan Velasco Alvarado (1968–1975). In den 1980ern verlagerte sich sein Augenmerk zunehmend auf Identitätsfragen und die Kritik an der europäischen Moderne. Diese Argumentation verdichtete sich schließlich in den 1990er Jahren in seinem Konzept der Kolonialität der Macht. Das Werk von Quijano hat sich entlang der Linien soziologischer lateinamerikanischer Debatten entwickelt und diese zugleich aufgegriffen und vorangetrieben. Es handelt sich um keine klar abgrenzbare und abstrakte Theorie, sondern um einen facettenreichen theoretischen Entwurf, der die Spezifika der postkolonialen Situation Perus deutlich macht und revolutionäre Perspektiven zeigt (Quijano 2020). Mehr als eine Theorie der Moderne, befasst sich das Werk Quijanos und seiner Zeitgenoss:innen mit der historisch-strukturellen Frage der abhängigen ökonomischen und kulturellen Entwicklung Lateinamerikas. In der hierzulande späten (Neu-)Entdeckung Quijanos als dekolonialer Theoretiker wird auch oft übersehen, dass es bereits eine Phase der internationalen Quijano-Rezeption gab. In den 1970er Jahren gehörte er zu den am häufigsten übersetzten und zitierten lateinamerikanischen Autor:innen, die im Kontext der Rezeption dependenztheoretischer Ansätze Aufmerksamkeit erfahren haben (Ruvituso 2020b).

Lateinamerika im Regenbogen-Regal: die *Dependencia*-Rezeption

Die *Dependencia*-Theorien gehören zu den einflussreichsten wissenschaftlichen Reaktionen auf die koloniale Erfahrung und deren Folgen in Lateinamerika und standen für die Konstruktion einer Gesellschaftstheorie aus der Peripherie. Die Debatten um die *Dependencia* prägten soziale Bewegungen des Nordens und Südens ebenso wie die kritische Agenda der Entwicklungspolitik weltweit und sie entwickelten sich parallel und in Verbindung mit den Theologien und Philosophien der Befreiung. Die *dependentistas* plädierten für eine Perspektive der Weltordnung aus Sicht der asymmetrischen Beziehungen zwischen Zentrum und Peripherie und damit für eine radikale Umkehr des Modernisierungsansatzes: Die Unterentwicklung wurde nicht länger als eine Art Übergangsphase der Länder der Dritten Welt angesehen, sondern als Resultat eines historischen Prozesses der ungleichen Integration in den kapitalistischen Weltmarkt im Rahmen des Kolonialismus und Imperialismus (Beigel 2015; Svampa 2016). Insbesondere forschten Soziolog:innen über differenzierte soziale Schichten im peripheren Kapitalismus, das Phänomen der »Marginalität«, die Besonderheiten der peripheren Stadtentwicklungen (»Slums«), die agrarischen Produktionsweisen und ihre ethnischen Dimensionen sowie die Problematisierung des sogenannten internen Kolonialismus. Auch das Phänomen des Populismus und Autoritarismus wurde dabei diskutiert. Mit der Entwicklungs-, Wirtschafts-, Arbeits-, Agrar- und Stadtsoziologie gibt es gleich mehrere Teildisziplinen der Soziologie, in denen die *Dependencia*-Ansätze signifikante Spuren hinterlassen haben. Die Zirkulation dieser Ansätze in der BRD entwickelte sich im Kontext der langfristigen politischen und kulturellen Veränderungen, die durch die 1967/68er-Bewegung und den Kalten Krieg geprägt waren. Zwei kongruente Faktoren trieben die Rezeption lateinamerikanischer Theorien an: die Gründung akademischer und politischer Institutionen mit dem Schwerpunkt Lateinamerika und die damit verbundene Förderung der Mobilität des wissenschaftlichen Nachwuchses zwischen Lateinamerika und der damaligen Bundesrepublik. Insbesondere Chile – das transregionale Zentrum der *Dependencia*-Debatte bis zum Pinochet-Putsch am 11. September 1973 – stand im Mittelpunkt der Begegnung westdeutscher und lateinamerikanischer Intellektueller. Die Lateinamerikaforschung wuchs ab Mitte der 1960er Jahre dezentral und autonom an verschiedenen Universitäten und Instituten, darunter Münster, Bielefeld, West-Berlin, Hamburg, Köln, Freiburg, Augsburg, Erlangen-Nürnberg, Eichstätt-Ingolstadt und Tübingen (Ruvituso 2019). In der BRD ermöglichte zudem die Gründung von parteinahen Stiftungen mit zunehmender Präsenz in Lateinamerika sowie von verschiedenen Institutionen der sogenannten Entwicklungshilfe[3] eine Erhöhung der Ressourcen für die Auseinandersetzung mit dem damals als Dritte Welt bezeichneten (Groß-)Teil der Welt. Das Interesse an der Dritten Welt wurde hier von einer Reihe breiter gesellschaftlicher Akteur:innen begleitet und befeuert – von der Sozialdemokratie über die Kirchen bis hin zu antiimperialistischen Bewegungen (Puhle 2018). Die *Dependencia* lieferte ihnen zentrale Argumente unter anderem für die kritische Diskussion um eine neue internationale Wirtschaftsordnung und um die Rolle der westlichen Entwicklungshilfe in der Dritten Welt. Seit 1968 waren verschiedene westdeutsche

3 später Entwicklungszusammenarbeit.

Verlage wie EVA, der Peter Hammer Verlag, Hoffmann und Campe, Suhrkamp und Wagenbach sowie linksorientierte Zeitschriften an der Platzierung lateinamerikanischer Themen und am Übersetzungsprozess der Werke lateinamerikanischer Autor:innen beteiligt. Insbesondere die Präsenz Lateinamerikas in der einflussreichen edition suhrkamp veränderte die bis dato asymmetrische Wissenszirkulation zugunsten der *dependentistas*. Vermittler:innen dieser Publikationen waren das deutsch-venezolanische Soziologie-Paar Heinz-Rudolf Sonntag und Elena Hochman und der Politologe Dieter Senghaas (Ruvituso 2020b). So fanden kaum bekannte venezolanische Autoren wie die Ökonomen Héctor Silva Michelena, Armando Córdova und Orlando Araujo und das soziologische Denken des kolumbianischen Revolutionärs Camilo Torres einen Platz im einflussreichen Regenbogen-Regal der edition und damit außergewöhnliche Verbreitung. Durch die Vermittlung von Sonntag gelangte zudem der Brasilianer Darcy Ribeiro mit »Der zivilisatorische Prozess« 1971 als einziger Lateinamerikaner in Suhrkamps Theorie-Reihe. Ribeiro teilte die zentralen Thesen der *Dependencia*, entwickelte aber darüber hinaus eine radikale Kritik an den epistemischen Beziehungen zwischen Zentren und Peripherien, dem Eurozentrismus des Marxismus sowie der Kritischen Theorie (Ruvituso 2021). Damit plädierte Darcy Ribeiro für eine Vertiefung der *Dependencia*-Ansätze im Sinne einer Thematisierung der Narrative der Moderne, der aktuellen Folgen des Kolonialismus und vor allem der Stimmen und des Wissens der Indigenen. Trotz der breiten Zirkulation von Ribeiros Werken in der Bundesrepublik der 1970er und 1980er Jahre und seiner wegweisenden Forschung zu Kolonialismus, Modernität und Zivilisation geriet er als Vordenker des Postkolonialismus in Vergessenheit. Dies gilt auch für den Peruaner José Carlos Mariátegui, einem der bedeutendsten und vielleicht am stärksten rezipierten kritischen Intellektuellen Lateinamerikas. Er befasste sich insbesondere mit der Frage, wie ethnische und Klassenkonflikte zusammenhängen und wie kolonialistische Abhängigkeitsstrukturen und der Dualismus von postkolonialem Feudalismus und indigener Kultur zu überwinden und eine inklusive neue peruanische Nationalkultur (*Peruanidad*) geschaffen werden kann. Mit seinen »Sieben Versuche[n], die peruanische Wirklichkeit zu verstehen«[4] entwickelte Mariátegui einen unorthodoxen marxistischen Ansatz, der unter anderem durch die Arbeit der Soziologin Eleonore von Oertzen in den westdeutschen Diskursraum gebracht wurde (Mariátegui, von Oertzen 1986). Insgesamt waren für die westdeutsche Rezeption der *Dependencia* die im Jahr

4 »Siete ensayos de interpretacion de la realidad peruana« (Mariátegui 1928).

1972 und 1974 veröffentlichten Sammelbände von Dieter Senghaas relevant: »Imperialismus und strukturelle Gewalt, Analysen über abhängige Reproduktion« und »Peripherer Kapitalismus. Analysen über Abhängigkeit und Unterentwicklung«, in denen Übersetzungen verschiedener Autoren der *Dependencia*-Debatte versammelt wurden. Dazu gehören Texte der Brasilianer Ruy Mauro Marini, Celso Furtado, Fernando Henrique Cardoso und Theotônio dos Santos, des Chilenen Osvaldo Sunkel, des Peruaners Aníbal Quijano und des Mexikaners Rodolfo Stavenhagen.[5] Der *Dependencia*-Ansatz wurde zudem in vielfältigen Lehr- und Forschungsprojekten in der Bundesrepublik angewandt. Hervorzuheben ist das 1971 gegründete Lateinamerika-Institut, das in Kooperation mit anderen Instituten der Freien Universität Berlin vergleichende Länder- und Regionalforschung betrieb, die heute größtenteils einer themengeleiteten Agenda gewichen ist, die Lateinamerika und die Karibik in (trans-)regionalen und globalen Verflechtungen untersucht: Quijano und Cardoso gehören seit jeher zu einflussreichen Referenzen in Berlin (Ruvituso 2020b).

Der Einfluss der *Dependencia*-Debatten lässt sich auch an der Entwicklung neuer Ansätze etwa in der Bielefelder Entwicklungssoziologie ablesen: In der internationalen Debatte wird bis heute insbesondere der Ansatz von Maria Mies zur Hausfrauisierung und Akkumulation von Kapital stark rezipiert (Boatcă 2015, Ojeda et al. 2022; vgl. unter anderem Mies 1986). Die Bielefelder:innen diskutierten das Konzept der »Marginalität« und beleuchteten die Rolle der Arbeit von Frauen in der kapitalistischen Akkumulation.[6] Kurz zuvor führte die Gruppe um Folker Frödel, Jürgen Heinrich und Otto Kreye am Starnberger Max-Planck-Institut zur Erforschung der Lebensbedingungen der wissenschaftlich-technischen Welt Forschungen im Dialog mit André Gunder Frank, Ruy Mauro Marini und Osvaldo Sunkel durch, die der Frage einer neuen internationalen Arbeitsteilung nachgingen (vgl. unter anderem Fröbel et al. 1973).

Obwohl die *Dependencia*-Ansätze unter dem Vorzeichen globaler Umordnungen in den 1980er Jahren ihre Zentralität verloren und Teil der (selbst-)kritischen Auseinandersetzung mit marxistischer Theorie und Politik wurden (Menzel 1992), haben sie dependenz- und weltsystemtheoretische Weiterentwicklungen erfahren (Martins 2022; Grosfoguel, Cervantes-Rodríguez 2002).

5 Unübersehbar ist, dass auch die *Dependencia*-Rezeption ein Genderproblem hat.

6 Neben Maria Mies auch Claudia von Werlhof und Veronika Bennholdt-Thomsen; für die Karibik siehe Reddock (1983).

Die regionalwissenschaftlichen »todologos« und ihr stiefmütterliches Dasein

Der für die Selbstreflexion notwendige Blick auf die Soziologie wird ungleich komplexer, wenn er sich nicht nur auf die transatlantische Wissenszirkulation im Hinblick auf prominente Stränge der kritischen Theorie richtet, sondern auf die Gesamtheit des multiparadigmatischen und in unzählige Spezialsoziologien aufgefächerten Faches. Wir haben die *Dependencia* als jenen facettenreichen Ansatz der kritischen lateinamerikanischen Theorie hervorgehoben, der für eine relationale, dezentrierte und vernetzte globale Soziologie auch gegenwärtig höchst relevant wird.[7] Mit dieser Hervorhebung ist jedoch zugleich eine Ausblendung verbunden, derer wir uns bewusst sind: Für die soziologische Beschäftigung mit Lateinamerika und der Karibik war und ist ein viel breiteres Spektrum an Theorien und Ansätzen relevant, als wir in der Kürze dieses Beitrags darstellen können. Wir haben uns auf die Dependenztheorien und das Œuvre Quijanos als Beispiele einer »epistemischen Revolte« (Costa 2023: 170) fokussiert, deren historische Zirkulation in den gegenwärtigen Diskussionen oft unterschlagen wird. Gleichzeitig kann von einer in sich geschlossenen Subdisziplin – einer Soziologie Lateinamerikas und der Karibik – keine Rede sein: Wie in der Soziologie insgesamt ist die Beschäftigung mit einer ganzen Weltregion und ihren transregionalen und globalen Verflechtungen thematisch und methodisch zu breit, als dass neben dem geteilten regionalen Interesse und dem Wissen um seine stiefmütterliche Behandlung in der Gesamtdisziplin subdisziplinäre Spezifika ausgemacht werden könnten (s. auch Costa 2023: 166 f.). Klaus Meschkat sagte in einem Interview 2008, dass ab einem bestimmten Zeitpunkt »zu einem ordentlichen soziologischen Institut auch Wissenschaftler gehör[t]en, die sich mit der außereuropäischen Welt beschäftigen« (Meschkat, Gabbert 2008: 34). Der konkrete geographische Bezug sei jedoch oft beliebig gewesen:

> »Und aus dieser ›Nischenexistenz‹ hat sich dann im Allgemeinen an solchen Instituten eine Art freundliche Koexistenz entwickelt. Man hat diese ›merkwürdigen Menschen‹, die dann natürlich ihre Arbeitsbezüge woanders suchen mussten, weil das im Rahmen der normalen Kommunikation mit den unmittelbaren Kollegen nicht intensiv stattfand, im besten Falle gewähren lassen«. (ebd.: 35).

7 Siehe auch die Beiträge zu Kritischer Theorie und Globaler Soziologie in der dritten Ausgabe von *Global Dialogue* (Lessenich et al. 2023).

Je nach politischer Couleur waren diese Arbeitsbezüge die revolutionären und emanzipatorischen Bewegungen Lateinamerikas, die dortigen Kolleg:innen aus der akademischen Welt und/oder die interdisziplinären Kontexte der Area Studies. Achim Schrader hat Anfang der 1990er Jahre 76 Personen in den Kanon seiner »indizierten Bibliographie« der soziologischen Lateinamerikaforschung aufgenommen (Schrader 1993). Nun sind die meisten der dort Versammelten gewiss keine Vorreiter:innen der dekolonialen Debatten der Gegenwart, doch sie stehen für eine Gruppe deutscher Wissenschaftler:innen, für die die Rezeption außereuropäischer Theorie schon immer eine Selbstverständlichkeit war. Die Zahl derer, die in der Nachkriegsgeschichte der Soziologie über den euro-nordamerikanischen Tellerrand geschaut haben,[8] ist gar nicht so klein. In der deutschen Wissenschaftslandschaft wurden aus diesen interdisziplinär arbeitenden Soziolog:innen oft »todologos« (Werz 2019): Gemeint sind damit flexible Allzweckwaffen, die zu einem breiten Themenspektrum publizierten und oft politiknahe Forschung betrieben – im Sinne emanzipatorischer oder revolutionärer Bewegungen, im Auftrag von staatlichen Institutionen oder in Kooperation mit parteinahen Stiftungen.

Fazit: Für eine Globale Soziologie

In Deutschland wie auch andernorts ist es zunehmend *en vogue*, den Kanon der Soziologie kritisch zu befragen und um (queer-)feministische, (post-)migrantische sowie post-, de- und antikoloniale Stimmen zu erweitern. Die historischen Bedingungen dieser Infragestellung sind die politischen Aushandlungen von Anerkennung, sozialer Gerechtigkeit und Teilhabe in der postmigrantischen und postkolonialen Gesellschaft, deren Verfasstheit sich am besten intersektional analysieren lässt. Aus der Perspektive soziologischer Lateinamerika- und Karibikforschung ergibt sich für uns die Frage: Welche Antworten hält die deutschsprachige Soziologie auf Fragen parat, die gar nicht erst gestellt werden? Viele Fragen entziehen sich der hiesigen soziologischen Phantasie (Mills 1959) globaler Reichweite und entsprechen gar nicht erst dem Selbstverständnis des soziologischen Arbeitsbereichs. Neben der gegenwärtigen systematischen Gewalt gegen Menschen, die nicht dem Weltbild weißer Vorherrschaft und des Heteropatriarchats entsprechen,

8 … und haben schauen können, denn dies ist auch immer eine Frage der Finanzierung.

wird auch ganzen historischen Episoden sozialen Wandels wie dem transatlantischen Handel mit versklavten Menschen, der Haitianischen Revolution und späteren Unabhängigkeitskämpfen sowie den vergangenen Militärdiktaturen und gegenwärtigen Rechtspopulismen in Lateinamerika und der Karibik kaum Aufmerksamkeit geschenkt. Jüngere bibliographische Ausnahmen im Feld der Soziologie sozialer Ungleichheiten bestätigen diese Regel (unter anderem Backhouse et al. 2021; Boatcă, Roth 2016; Costa 2020; Gutiérrez Rodríguez, Reddock 2021; Jelin, Motta, Costa 2017; Jenss, Lehmann, Boos 2021).

Eine kritische Soziologie, die diese Fragen aufgreift und auf die Produktion und Transformation von Strukturen der sozialen Ungleichheit zuspitzt, sollte in der Welt des 21. Jahrhunderts zwangsläufig eine globale sein. Zwar zeigen Publikationen und Konferenzprogramme ebenso wie kollaborative Forschungsplattformen wie das DFG-Netzwerk zu global ausgerichteter, qualitativer Sozialforschung,[9] dass der analytische Fokus auf die »eigene« Gesellschaft begonnen hat aufzuweichen : die Verschränkung der Soziologie mit der Sozial- und Kulturanthropologie zugunsten einer Verortung des Globalen Südens in der Theorielandschaft findet in ausgewählten Feldern längst statt und braucht dort kaum noch die Begründung, die vor einem Vierteljahrhundert vorgetragen werden musste (Randeria 1999). Allerdings bleibt bei der »(Selbst-)Reflexion über die materiell-strukturelle wie kulturelle und metaphorische Ver-Ortung der eigenen soziologischen Praxis« (Reuter, Villa 2010: 13) noch immens viel zu tun. Ein elementarer Bestandteil dieser Selbstreflexion ist die Aufweichung des dominanten Kanons auch im Sinne der (Wieder-)Entdeckung einer langen Geschichte der Wissenszirkulation zwischen Lateinamerika und Europa. Damit entsteht der »Anspruch einer globalen Soziologie, die sozialen Wandel hier wie dort – im lebensweltlich erfahrbaren Nahraum oder in entfernteren sozialen Gefilden – zu verstehen und in ihren wechselseitigen Abhängigkeiten sichtbar zu machen sucht« (Dobelmann, Oettler, Sott 2016: 182). Dass es Überschneidungen des vermeintlich Nahen und Fernen gibt, zeigt die wachsende Beschäftigung mit Europas Außengrenzen in Lateinamerika und der Karibik (Boatcă 2021, Santos 2022; Santos, Boatcă 2023) – und weist damit nur einen von vielen Wegen auf, den Kanon und die methodologischen Schieflagen der Disziplin herauszufordern. Zu lange hat die Soziologie ihre Relevanz jenseits eines minimalen Ausschnitts auf der Weltkarte aufs Spiel gesetzt – trotz ihrer an-

9 https://global-qualitative-sociology.net.

fänglichen globalen Rahmung (Connell 2007) und ihres hier im Beitrag deutlich gemachten episodenhaften Interesses an den materialistischen und ideologiekritischen Perspektiven, die in Lateinamerika entwickelt wurden.

Literatur

Backhouse, Maria / Lehmann, Rosa / Lorenzen, Kristina / Lühmann, Malte / Puder, Janina / Rodríguez, Fabricio / Tittor, Anne (eds.) 2021: Bioeconomy and Global Inequalities: Socio-Ecological Perspectives on Biomass Sourcing and Production. Cham: Palgrave Macmillan.

Beigel, Fernanda 2015: Das Erbe des lateinamerikanischen Dependentismo und die Aktualität des Begriffs der Abhängigkeit. Journal für Entwicklungspolitik, 31. Jg., Heft 3, 11–38.

Beigel, Fernanda / Packer, Abel L. / Gallardo, Osvaldo / Salatino, Maximiliano 2024a: OLIVA: The Scientific output in journals edited in Latin America. Disciplinary Diversity, Institutional Collaboration, and Multilingualism in SciELO and Redalyc (1995–2018). Dados, vol. 67, no. 1, 1–39.

Beigel, Fernanda et al. 2024b: OLIVA-2: las revistas iberoamericanas indexadas en Biblat y Latindex: fuentes fundamentales para conocer la producción científica global. e-Ciencias de la Información, vol. 14, no. 1, 1–22.

Boatcă, Manuela 2015: Global Inequalities Beyond Occidentalism. Farnham: Ashgate.

Boatcă, Manuela 2021: Thinking Europe Otherwise: Lessons from the Caribbean. Current Sociology, vol. 69, no. 3, 389–414.

Boatcă, Manuela / Costa, Sérgio 2010: Postkoloniale Soziologie: ein Programm. In Julia Reuter / Paula-Irene Villa (Hg.), Postkoloniale Soziologie. Bielefeld: transcript, 69–90.

Boatcă, Manuela / Farzin, Sina / Go, Julian 2018: E-Mail-Debate: Postcolonialism and Sociology. SOZIOLOGIE, vol. 47, no. 4, 423–438.

Boatcă, Manuela / Roth, Julia 2016: Unequal and gendered: Notes on the coloniality of citizenship. Current Sociology, vol. 64, no. 2, 191–212.

Bogusz, Tanja 2018: Ende des methodologischen Nationalismus? Soziologie und Anthropologie im Zeitalter der Globalisierung. SOZIOLOGIE, 47. Jg., Heft 2, 143–156.

Braig, Marianne / Ferdinand, Ursula / Zapata, Martha (Hg.) 1997: Begegnungen und Einmischungen: Festschrift für Renate Rott zum 60. Geburtstag. Stuttgart: Heinz.

Connell, Raewyn 2007: The Northern Theory of Globalization. Sociological Theory, vol. 25, no. 4, 368–385.

Costa, Sérgio 2020: Der Rechtsruck in Brasilien: Ein intersektionaler Deutungsversuch. Leviathan, 48. Jg., Heft 4, 655–679.

Costa, Sérgio 2023: Die Soziologische Lateinamerikaforschung. In Miriam Lay Brander (Hg.), Einführung in die Lateinamerikastudien. Berlin: Erich Schmidt, 165–182.

Curato, Nicole 2013: A Sociological Reading of Classical Sociological Theory. Philippine Sociological Review, vol. 61, no. 2, 265–287.

Dobelmann, Anna / Oettler, Anika / Sott, Sarah 2016: Decolonize ourselves? Über die Ambivalenz postkolonialer Verortungen. In Karolina Dreit / Nina Schumacher / Anke Abraham (Hg.), Ambivalenzen der Normativität in feministisch–kritischer Wissenschaft. Sulbach: Ulrike Helmer Verlag, 159–187.

do Mar Castro Varela, María / Dhawan, Nikita (Hg.) 2015: Postkoloniale Theorie. Eine kritische Einführung. Bielefeld: Transcript.

Fröbel, Folker / Heinrichs, Jürgen / Kreye, Otto / Sunkel, Osvaldo 1973: Internationalisierung von Kapital und Arbeitskraft. Leviathan, 1. Jg., Heft 4, 429–454.

Gingras, Yves / Mosbah-Natanson, Sebastien 2010: Where are social sciences produced? In International Social Science Council, UNESCO (ed.), World Social Science Report: Knowledge Divides. Paris: UNESCO Publishing/International Social Science Council, 149–153.

Grosfoguel, Ramón / Cervantes-Rodríguez, Ana Margarita (eds.) 2002: The Modern/Colonial/Capitalist World-System in the Twentieth Century: Global Processes, Antisystemic Movements, and the Geopolitics of Knowledge. Westport: Greenwood Press.

Gutiérrez Rodríguez, Encarnación / Reddock, Rohda (eds.) 2021: Decolonial Perspectives on Entangled Inequalities. Europe and The Caribbean. London: Anthem Press.

Jelin, Elizabeth / Motta, Renata C. / Costa, Sérgio (eds.) 2018: Global Entangled Inequalities: Conceptual Debates and Evidence from Latin America. Abingdon: Routledge.

Jenss, Alke / Lehmann, Rosa / Boos, Tobias 2021: Sozialstrukturen in Lateinamerika: Dynamiken und Akteure im 21. Jahrhundert. Wiesbaden: Springer VS.

Koloma Beck, Teresa 2018: Aufruf zum Aufstand. Diversität als wissenschaftliches Problem. Mittelweg 36, 27. Jg., Heft 3, 75–91.

Lessenich, Stephan / Bhambra, Gurminder K. / Boatcă, Manuela / Cipollitti Rodríguez, Patricia / de la Torre de C. Lima, Bruna 2023: The World According to Critical Theory (and Vice Versa). Global Dialogue, vol. 13, no. 3, 16–27.

Mariátegui, José Carlos 1928: Siete Ensayos de Interpretación de la Realidad Peruana. Lima: Empresa Editora Amauta.

Mariátegui, José Carlos / von Oertzen, Eleonore 1986: Revolution und peruanische Wirklichkeit. Frankfurt am Main: isp-Verlag.

Martins, Carlos Eduardo 2022: The Longue Durée of the Marxist Theory of Dependency and the Twenty-First Century. Latin American Perspectives, vol. 49, no. 1, 18–35.

Menzel, Ulrich 1992: Das Ende der Dritten Welt und das Scheitern der großen Theorie. Frankfurt am Main: Suhrkamp.

Meschkat, Klaus 2010: Konfrontationen. Streitschriften und Analysen 1958–2020. Hannover: offizin.

Meschkat, Klaus / Gabbert, Wolfgang 2008: Gesellschaften in Bewegung. Über die Geschichte und Gegenwart der lateinamerikabezogenen Soziologie. Interviewt von Anika Oettler, Lateinamerika Analysen, Heft 21, 31–46.

Mies, Maria 1986: Patriarchy and Accumulation on a World Scale: Women in the International Division of Labour. London: Zed Books.

Mills, C. Wright 1959: The Sociological Imagination. Oxford: Oxford University Press.

Ojeda, Diana / Nirmal, Padini / Rocheleau, Dianne / Emel, Jody 2022: Feminist Ecologies. Annual Review of Environment and Resources, vol. 47, no. 1, 149–171.

Pollock, Griselda 1999: Differentiating the Canon. Feminist Desire and the Writing of Art's Histories. London: Routledge.

Puhle, Hans-Jürgen 2018: Between Academia and Politics. Latin American Studies in Germany during the Cold War. Latin American Perspectives, vol. 45, no. 4, 69–97.

Quijano, Aníbal 2020: Cuestiones y horizontes: de la dependencia histórico-estructural a la colonialidad/descolonialidad del poder. CLACSO. https://doi.org/10.2307/j.ctv1gm019g.

Randeria, Shalini 1999: Jenseits von Soziologie und soziokultureller Anthropologie: Zur Ortsbestimmung der nichtwestlichen Welt in einer zukünftigen Sozialtheorie. Soziale Welt, 50. Jg., Heft 4, 373–382.

Reddock, Rhoda E. 1983. Frauen und Sklaverei in der Karibik. Beiträge zur feministischen Theorie und Praxis, 6. Jg., Heft 9/10, 125–134.

Reuter, Julia / Villa, Paula Irene 2010: Provincializing Soziologie. Postkoloniale Theorie als Herausforderung. In Julia Reuter / Paula Irene Villa (Hg.), Postkoloniale Soziologie. Empirische Befunde, theoretische Anschlüsse, politische Intervention. Bielefeld: transcript, 11–46.

Rivera Cusicanqui, Silivia 2019: Ch'ixinakax utxiwa: A Reflection on the Practices and Discourses of Decolonization. In Fernanda Beigel (ed.), Key Texts for Latin American Sociology. Los Angeles: SAGE, 290–306.

Ruvituso, Clara 2019: Sozialwissenschaftliche Lateinamerikaforschung in der BRD. In Nikolaus Werz / Günther Maihold / Hartmut Sangmeister (Hg.), Lateinamerika: Handbuch für Wissenschaft und Forschung. Baden-Baden: Nomos, 93–102.

Ruvituso, Clara 2020a: From the South to the North: The reception on dependency theories in the Federal Republic of Germany. Current Sociology, vol. 68, no. 1, 22–40.

Ruvituso, Clara 2020b: Southern theories in Northern circulation: analyzing the translation of Latin American dependency theories into German. Tapuya: Latin American Science, Technology and Society, vol. 3, no. 1, 92–106.

Ruvituso, Clara 2021: Southern Theories und die Öffnung des sozialwissenschaftlichen Kanons: Darcy Ribeiro's (vergessener) Beitrag zur Gesellschaftstheorie. Leviathan, 49. Jg., Heft 2, 266–285.

Sandner, Gerhard / Steger, Hanns-Albert (Hg.) 1973: Lateinamerika. Frankfurt am Main: Fischer.

Santos, Fabio 2022: Bridging Fluid Borders. Entanglements in the French-Brazilian Borderland. Abingdon: Routledge.

Santos, Fabio / Boatcă, Manuela 2023: European Elsewheres: Global Sociologies of Space and Europe. In Dominik Bartmanski / Henning Füller / Johanna Hoerning / Gunter Weidenhaus (eds.), Considering Space. A Critical Concept for the Social Sciences. Abingdon: Routledge, 136–158.

Santos, Fabio / Ruvituso, Clara (Hg.) 2024: Globale Soziologie. Verflochtene Geschichten, vergessene Theorien. Wiesbaden: Springer VS.

Schlichte, Klaus 2023: Indien gibt es nicht. Die Vernachlässigung Osteuropas steht für ein größeres Problem der deutschen Sozialwissenschaften. SOZIOLOGIE, 52. Jg., Heft 4, 415–424.

Schrader, Achim 1993: Soziologische Lateinamerika-Forschung: eine indizierte Bibliographie. Münster: Westfälische Wilhelms-Universität, Lateinamerika-Zentrum.

Senghaas, Dieter (Hg.) 1972: Imperialismus und strukturelle Gewalt, Analysen über abhängige Reproduktion. Frankfurt am Main: Suhrkamp.

Senghaas, Dieter (Hg.) 1974: Peripherer Kapitalismus. Analysen über Abhängigkeit und Unterentwicklung. Frankfurt am Main: Suhrkamp.

Svampa, Maristella 2016: La dependencia como eje organizador. In Maristella Svampa (ed.), Debates latinoamericanos: indianismo, desarrollo, dependencia y populismo. Buenos Aires: Edhasa, 137–192.

Werz, Nikolaus 2019: Die deutsche Lateinamerikaforschung im Wandel. In Peter Birle / Detlef Nolte (Hg.), 50 Jahre Arbeitsgemeinschaft Deutsche Lateinamerikaforschung ADLAF. Madrid, Frankfurt am Main: Vervuert, 103–125.

Worschech, Susann / Korablyova, Valeria / Langenohl, Andreas 2023: Symposion: Soziologische Perspektiven zu Osteuropa, Teil 1. SOZIOLOGIE, 52. Jg., Heft 3, 302–329.

Soziologie, 53. Jg., Heft 3, 2024, S. 320–327

Benötigt qualitative Forschung eine schriftliche Absicherung der Ethik?

Mathias Wagner

Forschung muss die selbst auferlegten und allgemein anerkannten Kriterien ethischen Verhaltens erfüllen. Für die Sozialforschung wie für jede Forschung mit Menschen gilt uneingeschränkt der Imperativ einer Abwehr von Schaden.[1] Die Aussage mag aufgrund ihrer Selbstverständlichkeit keiner Erörterung bedürfen und doch hat sich im Umgang mit Fragen der Forschungsethik seit ungefähr zehn Jahren ein Wandel vollzogen, der kritische Überlegungen provoziert.[2]

In der qualitativen Sozialforschung gehört die mündliche Zusicherung der Anonymisierung von Daten gegenüber den Akteuren in Interviews zum Standard. Während diese Praxis über Jahrzehnte anerkannt war, wurde sie mittlerweile durch schriftliche Vereinbarungen ersetzt. Würde man diese Veränderung jetzt schlicht als nebensächlich übergehen, versperrte man den Blick auf den Unterschied zwischen schriftlichen und mündlichen Äußerungen. Um die problematischen Aspekte deutlicher zu beschreiben, möchte ich die bisher übliche mündliche Praxis im Rahmen qualitativer Forschung skizzieren. Den Fokus lege ich auf Methoden ethnografischer Feldforschungen, da hierbei die Probleme in besonderem Maße sichtbar werden.

Der Kontakt zwischen Wissenschaftler_innen und Akteuren im Feld beruht in erster Linie auf wechselseitigem Vertrauen. Ohne Vertrauen werden Akteure nicht zu einem Interview einwilligen und einen Einblick in persönliche Sichtweisen, Probleme und Lebenszusammenhänge gewähren. Gleich-

---

1 Forschungsethische Fragen sind selbstverständlich nicht auf Arbeiten mit Menschen beschränkt.

2 Im Gegensatz dazu sieht von Unger den Diskurs zur Forschungsethik in einem »Winterschlaf« (von Unger 2014: 17).

zeitig vertrauen wir als Wissenschaftler_innen auf die ehrlichen und zumindest von kommerziellen Interessen freien Äußerungen unserer Interviewpartner_innen. Jeder Vergütung von unserer Seite wäre die Gefahr einer Steigerungslogik eigen, die Interviewpartner_innen zu möglichst passenden Erzählungen veranlassen könnte. Wie kommt es aber zu einem Vertrauensverhältnis zwischen Wissenschaftler_innen und Akteuren?

Das asymmetrische Verhältnis einer typischen Interviewsituation kann durch Vertrauen und Vertrautheit gemildert werden (vgl. Bourdieu 2005: 395). Beim Vertrauen handelt es um »ein[en] elementar[en] Tatbestand des sozialen Lebens« (Luhmann 2000: 1), der auf eine weitere Information zur Handlungsabsicherung verzichtet. In erster Linie entwickelt sich Vertrauen über lange Zeiträume und, wie Luhmann feststellt, über die Teilnahme am sozialen Leben (vgl. Luhmann 2000: 46, 80 f.). Simmel bezeichnet Vertrauen als »eine der wichtigsten synthetischen Kräfte innerhalb der Gesellschaft« (1992: 393). Vertrauen bildet eine Brücke »zwischen Wissen und Nichtwissen um einen Menschen« (ebd.), wobei es sich bei Vertrauen ausschließlich um ein Ergebnis sozialer Prozesse handelt. Vertrauen beruht eben gerade nicht auf manifestem Wissen oder rechtlicher Absicherung. Vielmehr wird eine komplexe Wirklichkeit »mit Hilfe symbolischer Implikationen kontrolliert« (Luhmann 2000: 36 f.). Möglich wird diese Brücke zwischen Wissen und Nichtwissen, weil die beteiligten Parteien davon ausgehen, dass sich beide an die üblichen Regeln halten (vgl. Sennett 2005: 55). Mit der mündlichen Zusicherung eines vertraulichen Umgangs mit den Informationen sowie der Anonymisierung der Daten beziehen sich beide Seiten auf eine im sozialen Leben übliche informelle Verhaltensnorm.

Vertrauen, so lässt sich resümieren, beruht zum einen auf der strikten Einhaltung eines erwartungsgemäß ehrlichen Umgangs mit Informationen. Zum anderen entwickelt sich Vertrauen aus subjektiven Merkmalen, die am ehesten als Sympathie zu beschreiben sind. »Man wird als teilnehmender Beobachter mehr akzeptiert wegen der Art der Person, als die man sich aus Sicht der Feldkontakte erweist, als der vermeintlichen Art der Forschung wegen« (Dean 1954: 233, zit. n. Girtler 2001: 94). Deutlich wird hier aber auch die notwendige Zeit als drittes Element. Begegnet man den Wissenschaftler_innen im Feld zunächst mit Distanz, vielleicht sogar mit Misstrauen, so wird sich dies in der Regel nach weiteren Begegnungen allmählich wandeln. Selbstverständlich ist damit noch nicht das Gelingen jedes Interviews sichergestellt. Denn eine Erfahrung der Feldforschung ist es, dass selbst redselige Personen, zu denen über Wochen ein Kontakt aufgebaut wurde, in Anbetracht eines Mikrophons verstummen. Auf der anderen Seite hat sich jedoch auch gezeigt, dass Interviewpartner_innen der Videoaufzeichnung eines Interviews zustimmen, nachdem ihnen die Verwendung zur Ausbildung von Studierenden erläutert wurde.

In den geschilderten Situationen vertraute man seit Jahrzehnten auf mündliche Zusagen, so wie für Wissenschaftler_innen die Verpflichtung zur Verschwiegenheit selbstverständlich war. Mittlerweile müssen die Studierenden, bevor sie im Rahmen des Studiums an einer Lehrforschung teilnehmen, eine Datenschutzerklärung unterzeichnen, die sie nicht nur zur Verschwiegenheit verpflichtet, sondern bei Zuwiderhandlungen mit Geld- oder Freiheitsstrafe droht. Das in juristischer Sprache verfasste Dokument führt bei Studierenden zu einer erheblichen Verunsicherung; dürfen Kommilito_ninnen das Interview lesen, muss ich alle Ortsangaben anonymisieren und so weiter.[3] In der Interviewsituation sind die Studierenden gehalten, den Interviewpartner_innen vorab ein einseitiges Dokument mit der wiederum im juristischen Deutsch formulierten Zusicherung eines vertraulichen Umgangs mit den Daten auszuhändigen. Bestätigt wird den Interviewpartner_innen die Freiwilligkeit ihrer Teilnahme und dass eine Nichtteilnahme keinerlei Nachteile für sie haben wird. Spätestens an dieser Stelle, so steht zu befürchten, wird manch ein unbedarfter Interviewpartner misstrauisch und mag sich fragen, ob er oder sie nicht doch etwas bei seiner Einwilligung übersehen hat. Durch den Hinweis auf Anonymisierung kommt es, wie Heiland und Lüdemann schreiben, zu der paradoxen Situation, dass Misstrauen geweckt wird (1993: 99). Doch unabhängig davon werden hier mit juristischer Drohgebärde schlicht der gesunde Menschenverstand beziehungsweise die ungeschriebenen Regeln sozialer Verhaltensweisen ad absurdum geführt. Wo hätte denn jemals bei einer qualitativen Forschung von Bronisław Malinowski über William Foote Whyte bis Sudhir Venkatesh die Verweigerung eines Interviews für die Akteure nachteilig sein können? Mit einem zweiten Dokument werden die Interviewpartner_innen aufgefordert, durch ihre Unterschrift die Zustimmung zu einem Interview zu bestätigen. Erst nach Unterzeichnung der Dokumente dürfen die Studierenden mit der Interviewaufzeichnung beginnen.

3 Im Einzelfall führte die Anonymisierung dazu, dass bei einer Studie zur Limmerstraße in Hannover nur noch von der Straße X in der Stadt Y gesprochen wurde. Ob aus der Studie überhaupt noch ein relevantes Resümee gezogen werden kann, bleibt unter diesen Bedingungen fraglich.

Man mag über diese Regelungen hinwegsehen, so wie die Mehrzahl der Interviewpartner_innen sich nicht die Mühe macht, ein mehrseitiges, in juristischer Sprache verfasstes Dokument zu lesen oder auch nur aufzubewahren. Wie sich zeigen lässt, machen wir es uns damit jedoch zu leicht. Vielmehr sollten wir uns fragen, welche Atmosphäre wir mit dieser Eröffnung für eine vertrauliche Interviewsituation schaffen. Wenn wir uns zunächst auf einer formalen Ebene bewegen, dann geben wir damit indirekt den Interviewpartner_innen ein Signal, in welcher Form sie den weiteren Gesprächsverlauf erwarten können. Es ist sicherlich nicht ausgeschlossen, doch noch zu einem von Vertrauen getragenen, narrativen Interviewstil zu finden, jedoch gilt es zunächst, die Kluft zwischen formalem Einstieg und narrativem Interviewbeginn zu überbrücken.

Als problematisch erweist sich dieser Einstieg bei Interviews mit vulnerablen Gruppen und Angehörigen sozialer Unterschichten. Ist es denkbar, eine Forschung zum Lebensalltag von Obdachlosen als Feldforschung durchzuführen, bei der ein Vertrauensverhältnis aufgebaut wurde und vor dem Interview juristische Dokumente zur Unterschrift vorgelegt werden? Denkbar sind zwei Szenarien. Entweder unterschreiben Akteure, weil ihr Vertrauen zu den Wissenschaftler_innen größer als ihr Misstrauen gegenüber behördlichen Texten ist, oder der Kontakt bricht ab. Zu der von Reichertz 2021 im Zusammenhang mit digitalen Interviewformaten angesprochenen Problematik der erforderlichen technischen Kompetenz auf Seiten der Interviewpartnerinnen und Interviewpartner kommt hier auch die Frage der Fähigkeit des Verständnisses komplexer Texte hinzu.

Noch eklatanter stellt sich die angesprochene Problematik, wenn wir uns in sozialen Gruppen mit kriminellen oder sozial geächteten Handlungsweisen bewegen. Man stelle sich vor, Sudhir Venkatesh hätte im Treppenhaus der »Lake Park Projects« J. T., wie er den Anführer einer Gang nennt, zunächst eine Vertraulichkeitserklärung übergeben und ihn um seine schriftliche Zustimmung gebeten (vgl. Venkatesh 2008: 28). Oder Roland Girtler hätte, als er sich in der Stehbierhalle des Wiener Westbahnhofs zu einer Gruppe Sandler stellte, diesen zunächst schriftlich den vertraulichen Umgang mit ihren Gesprächen zugesichert (vgl. Girtler 1996: 43 f.). Doch selbst verbreitete Handlungsweisen können soweit schambesetzt sein, dass Akteure den Kontakt mit Wissenschaftler_innen vermeiden. Wie der Autor in einer Feldforschung feststellte, war die Kontaktaufnahme zu Arbeitsmigrantinnen in deren polnischen Heimatdörfern nur möglich, wenn vorab ein persönliches Vertrauensverhältnis bestand. Obwohl im Zeitraum der Forschung die Arbeitsmigration nach Deutschland und anderen EU-Staaten legal war, erwies es sich als schwierig, Migrantinnen und Migranten für Interviews zu gewinnen.[4]

Im Vordergrund steht bei diesen Kontakten immer die persönliche Beziehung zwischen Wissenschaftler_innen und Akteuren. Meine These ist, dass die Einbeziehung der verschriftlichten juristischen Ebene nicht nur im Widerspruch zu einem von subjektiven Faktoren getragenem Vertrauensverhältnis steht, sondern sogar zu Misstrauen und zum Abbruch des Kontaktes führen kann. Günstigstenfalls werden die Schreiben schlicht als lästiges Beiwerk unterschrieben, ohne dem Inhalt weitere Beachtung zu schenken. In letzterem Fall müsste man aber einmal fragen, ob die Verschriftlichung eigentlich der Absicherung der Akteure oder nicht viel mehr der Wissenschaftler_innen dient? Sollte es jedoch zu einem Abbruch der Kontakte kommen, so steht zu befürchten, dass soziale Unterschichten immer weniger in qualitativen Forschungen eine Rolle spielen werden.

Eine konsequente Anwendung der Vorgaben führt in ethnografischen Feldforschungen zu der Frage, in welchem Umfang die Akteure zu informieren sind. Kommt doch bei dieser Methode gerade den informellen, mehr oder weniger nebenbei geführten Alltagsgesprächen[5] eine besondere Rolle zu. Oder kommen wir zu der Situation, dass Fragen gar nicht erst gestellt werden, die nicht durch datenschutzrechtliche Übereinkünfte abgesichert wurden? Wird hier ein formeller Rahmen vorgegeben, der dazu führt, »Halbgares und Informelles« (Reichertz 2021: 329) nicht auszusprechen? Qualitative Forschungsmethoden leben von der Nähe zwischen den Forschenden und den Akteuren. Nicht nur der Blickkontakt ist hier entscheidend, sondern die Forschenden sind mit ihrer gesamten Erscheinung und Persönlichkeit in den Forschungsprozess involviert. Auf dieser alltäglich-zwischenmenschlichen Ebene wird Vertrauen entwickelt und darf auf keinen Fall untergraben werden. Bei einer Verletzung des Vertrauens besteht tendenziell die Gefahr negativer Auswirkungen auch auf weitere Forschungen. Die Anonymisierung der Daten und die Abwehr eventuellen Schadens von den Akteuren steht unumstößlich über allen qualitativen Forschungen. Dieser Fixpunkt

4 Vermutlich spielten hier zwei Faktoren eine Rolle. Erstens hatten die Migrantinnen bis vor wenigen Jahren illegal in Deutschland gearbeitet und zweitens wurde ihnen von der katholischen Kirche eine Vernachlässigung ihrer Familie (Stichwort Eurowaisen) angelastet (vgl. Wagner 2013: 186 ff.).

5 Im Sinne von Girtler könnte man hier ero-epische Gespräche erwähnen (2001: 147 ff.).

gilt auch für Forschungen in informellen beziehungsweise illegalen Bereichen der Gesellschaft. Beispielsweise sei hier auf eine Forschung zum informellen Kleinhandel respektive Schmuggel an der EU-Ostgrenze verwiesen (vgl. Wagner 2011). In teilnehmender Beobachtung begleiteten Wissenschaftlerinnen und Wissenschaftler der Universitäten Bielefeld, Warschau und Kaliningrad russische und polnische Schmuggler auf deren Fahrten zwischen dem russischen Kaliningrad und der polnischen Wojewodschaft Ermland/Masuren. Bei der Klärung forschungsethischer Fragen vereinbarten die Wissenschaftler_innen Verschwiegenheit über Warenverstecke und Methoden der Schmuggler_innen. Mit dieser Absprache wurde eine wirtschaftliche Schädigung durch Weitergabe sensibler Informationen vermieden, ohne dass eine schriftliche Fixierung erfolgte. Vielmehr beruhte das Vertrauen der Schmuggler ausschließlich auf der individuellen persönlichen Erfahrung mit den Wissenschaftlerinnen und Wissenschaftlern. Vertrauen entstand durch das Verhalten der Wissenschaftlerinnen und Wissenschaftler, die, wie eine Schmugglerin es ausdrückte, Interesse an ihrem Leben hätten und sie oftmals auf ihren Fahrten begleiteten.

Vertraulichkeit begründete sich in den zitierten Beispielen im Verhalten der Wissenschaftlerinnen und Wissenschaftler, wurde mündlich vereinbart und von beiden Seiten für ausreichend angesehen. In einigen Fällen ist anzunehmen, dass die Verschriftlichung der Vereinbarungen die Forschung gestört oder sogar verhindert hätte. Grundsätzlich stellt sich aber die Frage, ob eine Verschriftlichung überhaupt sinnvoll ist. Wenn die Daten anonymisiert werden, können die Akteure aus Publikationen keinen Rückschluss auf einzelne Personen ziehen. Wen und in welcher denkbaren Konstellation soll man vor anonymisierten Daten schützen? Warum benötigen wir die schriftliche Zusicherung eines Einverständnisses? Meiner Ansicht nach geht es hier nur scheinbar um den Schutz der Akteure, vielmehr schützen wir Wissenschaftlerinnen und Wissenschaftler uns vor den Akteuren.

Wir bauen mit der schriftlichen Bestätigung juristischer Formalien eine akademische Distanz zu den Akteuren auf, die den üblichen sozialen Verhaltensweisen widerspricht. Dabei besteht die Gefahr, gerade Bevölkerungsgruppen mit geringer Bildung oder distanziertem Misstrauen gegenüber dem akademischen Betrieb aus dem Blick zu verlieren (vgl. Reichertz 2021: 316). Folglich laufen wir Gefahr, ein von allen Höhen und Tiefen geglättetes Bild der Realität zu präsentieren. Qualitative Forschung lebt jedoch von der empirischen Nähe und der fachlichen Kompetenz von Wissenschaftlerinnen und Wissenschaftlern, zugleich eine theoretische Distanz zu bewahren, die es ihnen ermöglicht, Motivationen und Handlungsweisen zu analysieren.

Es sollte deutlich geworden sein, dass die grundsätzliche Arbeitsweise einer Anonymisierung hier nicht infrage gestellt wird. Kritisch betrachtet wird dagegen die vorbehaltlose Übernahme formalisierter juristischer Kriterien in eine empirische Forschungspraxis, die von der Nähe zu alltäglichen Praktiken der Akteure lebt. Mit der Unterzeichnung schriftlicher Dokumente wird eine umfassende informierte Zustimmung vorgetäuscht, obwohl beide Seiten weder wissen, auf welche Inhalte sie sich bezieht, noch in welchen Situationen sie weitergegeben werden (vgl. auch Hopf 1991; Gläser 1999). Im Übrigen wird mit dem Beharren auf eine schriftliche Fixierung der Anonymisierung die in vergleichbarer Weise gültige, das heißt, einklagbare Form mündlicher Vereinbarungen ignoriert.[6] Zu klären wäre dann immer noch, in welchem Umfang eine Anonymisierung notwendig ist. Einen Orientierungspunkt liefert die Forderung, Einzelpersonen hinter Pseudonymen so zu verstecken, dass sie nicht oder nur mit erheblichem Aufwand und selbst dann nicht mit Sicherheit erkennbar sind. Gleichzeitig gilt es keine »blutleeren« Texte zu produzieren, bei denen Akteure zu Nummern und Örtlichkeiten zu Buchstaben werden und die lediglich von einem Fachpublikum gelesen werden.

Literatur

Bourdieu, Pierre 2005: Verstehen. In Pierre Bourdieu et al., Das Elend der Welt. Zeugnisse und Diagnosen alltäglichen Leidens an der Gesellschaft. Konstanz: Universitätsverlag, 393–426.

Dean, John P. 1954: Participant Observation and Interviewing. In John Th. Doby (ed.), An Introduction to Social Research. Harrisburg: Stackpole Co., 225–252.

Girtler, Roland 1996: Randkulturen. Theorie der Unanständigkeit. Wien, Köln, Weimar: Böhlau.

Girtler, Roland 2001: Methoden der Feldforschung. Wien, Köln, Weimar: Böhlau.

Gläser, Jochen 1999: Datenschutzrechtliche und ethische Probleme beim Publizieren von Fallstudien: Informantenschutz und ›Objektschutz‹. SOZIOLOGIE, 28. Jg., Heft 4, 32–47.

6 Laut der informellen Aussage einer Richterin haben mündliche Übereinkommen vor Gericht eine vergleichbare Relevanz wie schriftliche Abmachungen.

Heiland, Hans-Günther / Lüdemann, Christian 1993: Ein untauglicher Versuch soziologischer Moralbildung? Kritische Anmerkungen zum Ethik-Kodex. SOZIOLOGIE, 22. Jg., Heft 2, 97–110.

Hopf, Christel 1991: Zwischen Betrug und Wahrhaftigkeit – Fragen der Forschungsethik in der Soziologie. SOZIOLOGIE, 20. Jg., Heft 2, 174–191.

Luhmann, Niklas 2000: Vertrauen. Ein Mechanismus zur Reduktion sozialer Komplexität. Stuttgart: Lucius und Lucius.

Reichertz, Jo 2021: Die coronabedingte Krise der qualitativen Sozialforschung. SOZIOLOGIE, 50. Jg., Heft 3, 313–335.

Sennett, Richard 2005: Die Kultur des Neuen Kapitalismus. Berlin: Berlin Verlag.

Simmel, Georg 1992: Soziologie. Untersuchungen über die Formen der Vergesellschaftung. Frankfurt am Main: Suhrkamp.

Venkatesh, Sudhir 2008: Underground Economy. Was Gangs und Unternehmen gemeinsam haben. Berlin: Ullstein.

von Unger, Hella 2014: Forschungsethik in der qualitativen Forschung: Grundsätze, Debatten und offene Fragen. In Hella von Unger / Petra Narimani / Rosaline M'Bayo (Hg.), Forschungsethik in der qualitativen Forschung. Reflexivität, Perspektiven, Positionen. Wiesbaden: Springer, 15–39.

Wagner, Mathias 2011: Die Schmugglergesellschaft. Informelle Ökonomien an der Ostgrenze der Europäischen Union: Eine Ethnographie. Bielefeld: Transcript.

Wagner, Mathias 2013: »Meist merkt man, dass etwas geschehen ist« – die Kinder der Wanderarbeiter. In Mathias Wagner / Kamila Fiłkowska / Mara Piechowska / Wojciech Łukowski (Hg.), Deutsches Waschpulver und polnische Wirtschaft. Bielefeld: transcript, 183–207.

Transitionen

Themenpapier zum 42. Kongress der Deutschen Gesellschaft für Soziologie vom 22. bis 26. September 2025 auf dem Campus Duisburg der Universität Duisburg-Essen

Das Kongressthema: »Transitionen«

Unter dem Leitbegriff »Transitionen« stellen wir auf dem 42. Kongress der Deutschen Gesellschaft für Soziologie Prozesse sozialen Wandels zur Debatte. Die Soziologie als wissenschaftliche Disziplin wurde in Zeiten zum Teil rapider und fundamentaler gesellschaftlicher Umbrüche etabliert, sie hat seither verschiedene weitreichende gesellschaftliche Veränderungen kritisch reflektierend begleitet und hält entsprechend zahlreiche Begriffe zur Beschreibung solcher Phänomene bereit: sozialer *Wandel*, *Transformation*, *Prozess*, *Entwicklung*, *Evolution* oder auch *Revolution.* Mit dem Begriff der »Transitionen« als Leitbegriff für diesen Kongress sollen vor allem die *Verläufe und Dynamiken* gesellschaftlicher, institutioneller wie individueller Veränderungen in ihren unterschiedlichen Qualitäten fokussiert werden. Der Blick liegt damit stärker als in Konzeptionen des sozialen Wandels auf den Prozessen des Übergangs mit ihren Momenten des »Dazwischen«, der Kontingenz und der Offenheit wie auch möglicher Regelhaftigkeit, Regulierung und Gerichtetheit weiterer Entwicklungen. Soziale Transitionen beschreiben Zustände des Werdens; sie sind sowohl ein Nicht-Mehr als auch ein Noch-Nicht und können auf allen Ebenen des Sozialen und in allen Bereichen der Gesellschaft beobachtet werden. Im Mittelpunkt des Kongresses stehen somit weniger Phänomene der Konstanz und der Langlebigkeit, als vielmehr Soziales im Entstehen, in der Veränderung und im Übergang – Gesellschaft in und als Transitionen.

Facetten und Qualitäten von Transitionen

Soziale Phänomene der Transition sind ausgesprochen zahlreich und heterogen. Ihre Vielfalt interessiert soziologische Forschung und Theoriebildung auf verschiedene Weise:

1. Mit Blick auf die *Größenordnung und Reichweite* von Phänomenen des gesellschaftlichen Wandels sind Transitionen im Großen wie im Kleinen von soziologischem Interesse. Sie umfassen Prozesse, die parallel oder zeitversetzt verlaufen, die unterschiedlich weit ausgreifen und vielfältig miteinander verflochten sind. Transitionen sind Ausdruck von Veränderung und sie verändern das gesellschaftliche (Zusammen-)Leben und seine Strukturen auf verschiedenen Ebenen und zugleich über verschiedene Felder hinweg. Sie beziehen sich auf das soziale Geschehen im Politischen wie im Administrativen, im Alltäglichen wie im Strukturellen, im Religiösen wie im Ökonomischen, im subjektiven Erleben wie in technischen Objekten und Artefakten – und dies in differenter Weise, die oft neue Ungleichheiten hervorbringt. Digitalisierung ist zum Beispiel ein solcher tiefgreifender und umfassender Transitionsprozess, der alle gesellschaftlichen Bereiche zu erfassen sucht.

Phänomene *globaler und weltgesellschaftlicher Reichweite* wie der Klimawandel machen Fragen nach dem sozialen Umgang hiermit relevant, beispielsweise im Übergang zu nachhaltigeren Lebens- und Wirtschaftsweisen – einer Herausforderung, vor der alle Gesellschaften weltweit stehen. Dabei zeigt die Klimakrise eindrücklich, dass soziologische Forschungen multiperspektivisch entworfen werden müssen: Die jeweiligen Konstellationen auf den verschiedenen Ebenen, in denen Transitionen stattfinden und untersucht werden, erfordern die ganze Bandbreite des soziologischen Analyse-Instrumentariums. Um ein weiteres Beispiel anzuführen: Miteinander verflochtene kriegerische Konflikte können auf *supranationaler* Ebene als Elemente eines Übergangs in eine neue geopolitische Weltordnung beobachtet und so für die Soziologie Thema werden. Solche Wandlungsprozesse schlagen sich zugleich auf *nationalgesellschaftlicher* Ebene nieder, wo sie unter anderem im politischen Feld weitere Transitionsprozesse anstoßen können. Umgekehrt entfalten nationalgesellschaftliche Dynamiken Wirkungen auf supranationaler und globaler Ebene und bedingen zugleich weitere Entwicklungsdynamiken zum Beispiel in Familien, wenn kriegsbedingte Abwesenheiten einzelner Familienmitglieder neue Verteilungen von Aufgaben und Verantwortlichkeiten nach sich ziehen.

Neben globalen Fragen sind Nationalgesellschaften und -ökonomien mit weiteren, oft spezifisch auf dieser Ebene problematisierten Transitionen konfrontiert, wie etwa demografische Übergänge der sogenannten Baby-Boomer-Generation in die nacherwerbliche Lebensphase, die nicht nur im Hinblick auf den Fachkräftemangel eine Herausforderung etwa für die bundesrepublikanische (Post-)Migrationsgesellschaft darstellen. Diese gesamtgesellschaftlichen Vorgänge rapiden Wandels korrespondieren mit Veränderungen auf weiteren

Ebenen des Sozialen: Organisationen, Institutionen und Infrastrukturen (zum Beispiel Bürokratien oder Kommunikationsmedien und ihre Nutzungsarten) weisen je spezifische Transitionen auf. Zugleich werden Transitionen auf der mikrosozialen Ebene von *Interaktionen und dem individuellen Leben* relevant, wenn etwa Veränderungen größerer Reichweite zu Veränderungen sozialer Praktiken und der Formen sozialer Beziehungen führen. Daneben finden sich aber auch für diese Mikro-Ebene typische und genuin strukturelle Transitionen: Der gesellschaftlich und kulturell institutionalisierte Übergang zur Elternschaft oder die Transition zwischen Geschlechterkategorien sind oft einschneidende Übergangsphänomene, die im Privaten und Höchstpersönlichen genauso wirksam werden und soziologisch dort aufgesucht und untersucht werden müssen, wie sie umgekehrt auch mit Phänomenen größeren Maßstabs in ko-konstitutiven oder relativierenden Zusammenhängen stehen. Hier öffnet sich ein weites Feld möglicher theoretischer und empirischer Problemstellungen. Dazu zählt auch die Frage, wie Transitionen auf verschiedenen Ebenen (sei es individuell-biografisch, organisational, institutionell, feldspezifisch oder gesamtgesellschaftlich) in ihren vielfältigen Relationen und dynamischen Wechselwirkungen gedacht und untersucht werden können.

2. Mit Blick auf die *Form und Logik* von Transitionen werden Fragen der Geordnetheit und Geplantheit (sowie Plan*bar*keit) einerseits und der Offenheit, Kontingenz und Dynamik von Transitionen andererseits relevant. Wir laden ein, mit dem Begriff ›Transition‹ als Leitbegriff zur Analyse fortlaufender (das heißt historisch noch nicht abgeschlossener) Entwicklungen vor allem die Dynamik und Kontingenz entsprechender Vorgänge in den Vordergrund zu stellen und Sozialität als prinzipiell offen zu betrachten, also soziale Veränderungen ohne Rekurs auf teleologische Vorstellungen oder Zwangsläufigkeit zu denken. Das impliziert keineswegs soziologische Beliebigkeit, denn auch im Ungeplanten können sich Muster und (wiederholbare) Formen offenbaren. Gleichwohl können Transitionen auch geplant und organisiert sein, sodass sie ebenso Gegenstand von gesellschaftlichen Anstrengungen der Ordnung und Regelung sind. Da Transitionen in der Regel nicht ex nihilo entstehen, schreiben sie historisch gewachsene Strukturen fort – indem sie sie jedoch auch verändern oder gar mit ihnen brechen. Transitionen stellen potentiell konflikthafte oder doch zumindest konfliktaffine Prozesse dar, die in ihrer Form mit Blick auf Macht und Herrschaft zu diskutieren sind.

Soziologisch lassen sich mit dem Fokus auf Transitionen unvorhergesehene Ereignisketten ebenso rekonstruieren, wie erwartete Dynamiken empirisch untersucht oder Versuche der Modellierung von Zukunft unternommen werden. Der Blick auf Transitionen soll sich auf die Erfassung unsicherer und instabiler Übergänge genauso richten wie auf Bemühungen, solche Veränderungen zu antizipieren und explizit zu gestalten (oder im Nachhinein mit Sinn zu versehen). Im Kontrast zu teleologisch grundierten Prozessbegriffen (exemplarisch: Modernisierung) und der Gerichtetheit des Transformationsbegriffs wollen wir mit dem Begriff der Transitionen aber auch den Blick für das Offene, Unintendierte, Übergangshafte weiten.

Zugleich soll diese Perspektive dazu anregen, die innere Logik verschiedener Transitionen und ihrer Verknüpfungen zu reflektieren. Zu fragen ist zum Beispiel nach der Dynamik und Form von Transitionen: Wie vollziehen sich Transitionen praktisch und materiell? Mit welchen Verteilungs-, Ressourcen- und Machtfragen ist dies verbunden? Welche Vorstellungen von Neuem oder Altem werden (performativ) impliziert? Welche Wertvorstellungen und Bewertungen von ›schlechteren‹ oder ›besseren‹ Zuständen und Imaginationen eines ›davor‹ und ›danach‹ gehen mit Transitionen einher? Wie wird der Übergang lebensweltlich gedeutet, wie praktisch bewältigt, wie institutionell gespurt? Wie zeigen sich darin Differenzen, die über *Größenordnung und Reichweite* systematisch rekonstruiert werden können? Die Perspektive auf Transitionen erlaubt einen vergleichenden soziologischen Blick auf empirische Fälle solcher Veränderungen, auf ihre gegebenenfalls ungerichteten und dabei ambivalenten Dynamiken sowie auf ihre je eigenen Rhythmen, (Un-)Geregeltheiten und Abfolgen.

3. Die verschiedenen Qualitäten von Transitionen ergeben sich auch aus den (institutionellen wie alltäglichen) *Qualifizierungen, Rahmungen, Deutungen und Problematisierungen* entsprechender Phänomene. Sie werden immer auch auf diskursiver Ebene kommentiert und eingeordnet und damit als soziale Phänomene mithervorgebracht. Transitionen werden politisch und kulturell teils hoch emotional verhandelt. Solche Beschreibungen und Bewertungen von Transitionen sind Teil des Phänomens und zugleich eine Meta-Ebene, die soziologischer Untersuchung bedarf. Die historische und vergleichende Beschreibung gesellschaftlicher Veränderungen, das Bemühen um systematisches Verstehen, die Interpretation konkreter Prozesse wie diffus erscheinender Entwicklungen und die nüchternen Analysen sozialen Wandels gehören seit jeher zum Fach.

Gleiches gilt für die methodologische Reflexion der dabei verwendeten Begriffe, Konzepte und Methoden, um die gewünschte Distanz zur affektiven, subjektiven Wahrnehmung der Gesellschaft zu ermöglichen. So ließe sich etwa die Krisen- und Übergangsrhetorik selbst zum Gegenstand historisierender Perspektiven machen: Wie wurde in vergangenen Zeiten und wie wird aktuell eine gesellschaftliche Transitionszeit adressiert, inwieweit ist sie auf lokaler, nationaler oder globaler Ebene oder als Verbindung dazwischen zu verorten, welche Diskurse und Disziplinen sind dabei leitend und welche kollektiven Imaginationen werden auf diesen Ebenen sichtbar? In diesem Zusammenhang ist nicht zuletzt auch im Blick zu behalten, welche Aussagen zu wünschbaren gesellschaftlichen Veränderungen und welche normativen Kritiken sich von der Soziologie als wissenschaftlicher Disziplin verantworten lassen oder von ihr erwartet werden: Inwieweit sind Formen der gerechten Ausgestaltung von Übergängen (prominent etwa im Zusammenhang der Klimakrise) soziologisch begründungsfähig, und welche anderen Fragen von »transitional justice« geraten in den Blick, wenn sich die Soziologie hierbei nicht allein auf die Beschreibung und Untersuchung unterschiedlicher Gestaltungsabsichten zurückziehen will? Sind die aktuellen gesellschaftlichen Krisenbeschreibungen im Kern vom Fach mit angetriebene Rhetoriken (wie bereits mehrfach auf Soziologiekongressen diskutiert)? Und welche Macht entfalten diese und weitere uns eigenen Formen von Wissen?

Begriffe und Methoden soziologischer Analysen von Transitionen

Neben der Bearbeitung konkreter Phänomene von Transitionen soll der Kongress auch einen Rahmen für die Frage bieten, wie die Soziologie mit ihren Instrumenten gesellschaftliche Transitionen begrifflich und mithilfe unterschiedlicher Forschungsmethoden empirisch in den Blick nehmen kann.

1. Richtet man hier zunächst den Blick auf die Denkbarkeit und Intelligibilität von Transitionen, auf die *Konzepte und Begriffe,* so lässt sich aus dem 19. Jahrhundert kommend, am Anfang der Disziplin eine Dominanz oder Plausibilität evolutionistischer und teleologischer Theorien feststellen, die eine lineare beziehungsweise gerichtete Abfolge von Gesellschaften zu denken suchten, etwa in Stufen- oder Phasenmodellen gesellschaftlicher Entwicklung. Die Arbeiten der beiden Namensgeber des Faches, Herbert Spencer und Auguste Comte, hatten dabei eine enorme Wirkung; wie auch Karl Marx, Ferdinand Tönnies, Emile Durkheim, Max Weber oder später Talcott Parsons, die auf je eigene Weise nach ›Gesetzen‹ der Veränderung beziehungsweise Stabilität trotz vordergründiger Veränderungen von Gesellschaft suchten, etwa im

Sinne einer (letztlich kontinuierlichen und gerichteten, wenn auch ungeplanten) Modernisierung – je verstanden als Zivilisierung, Rationalisierung oder Differenzierung, oder als Folge von Klassenkämpfen. Diese Perspektiven laufen darauf hinaus, distinkte soziale Zustände zu diagnostizieren oder zu postulieren, *zwischen* denen ein Übergang stattfindet, wobei die Transition selbst oft eher nur sekundär interessiert.

Prozessperspektiven im engeren Sinne rücken dagegen die Permanenz und dabei die Unbestimmtheit, Kontingenz oder Unvorhersehbarkeit von sozialen Veränderungen ins Zentrum. Gesellschaftliche Zustände oder Ordnungen werden hier als (notwendige) gesellschaftliche Narrationen analysiert. Dies ist zum Beispiel angelegt in soziologischen Theorien der Post- beziehungsweise Spätmoderne, die gegenwärtige gesellschaftliche Entwicklungen zwar auch als Fortführungen oder Erweiterungen früherer Phasen gesellschaftlicher Entwicklung verstehen, dabei aber deren Offenheit und Ambivalenz betonen. Darüber hinaus ist an pragmatistische und an französische differenztheoretische Denktraditionen zu erinnern: Für diese sind allein Prozesse ständigen und unvorhersehbaren Anders-Werdens real, und gerade deshalb ist es gesellschaftlich notwendig, Ordnungen und Identitäten imaginär zu instituieren. Wie lassen sich in diesen und weiteren Denktraditionen Kontingenzen und Ambivalenzen von Vorgängen des Übergangs, von sozialen Verhältnissen *im Übergang* beschreiben? Welche Konzepte stehen dafür auch aus anderen Disziplinen zur Verfügung – etwa aus Geschichtswissenschaft, Philosophie, Erziehungswissenschaft, Kulturwissenschaften, Natur- und Lebenswissenschaften? Verschiedene Konzepte tragen unterschiedliche Vorstellungen der Qualitäten von Übergangsphasen mit sich. Die Begriffe sozialer Kipppunkte oder gesellschaftlicher Brüche betonen die begrenzte Kontrollierbarkeit von Übergängen und deren Plötzlichkeit. Demgegenüber stellen Konzepte wie Übergangsriten die Geordnetheit und gesellschaftliche Regulierung von biografischen Übergängen und ihre Folgen heraus. Weitere Begriffe, wie Liminalität oder Schwellenzustand, beschreiben zugleich einen unbestimmten Status von Individuen oder Kollektiven, in dem soziale Klassifizierungen noch nicht oder nicht mehr greifen.

2. Neben der Diskussion angemessener begrifflich-theoretischer Instrumente stellt sich ebenso die Frage nach der empirischen Beobachtbarkeit von Transitionen, nach geeigneten Verfahren der Datengenerierung und den damit verbundenen *methodischen Instrumenten* der empirischen Sozialforschung: Welche Methoden sind insgesamt geeignet, Veränderungen zu er-

fassen – zum Beispiel historische Vergleiche, Biografie- und Lebenslaufforschung, Diskursanalysen, die Erforschung historischer Semantiken, die Erhebung von Prozess- und Paneldaten, Zeitreihen- oder Kohortenanalysen? Welche Grenzen haben diese Methoden und Daten jeweils, und welche Artefakte werden damit erzeugt? Welche Weiter- und Neuentwicklungen wären hier notwendig und wie können sie angegangen werden? Wie verhalten sich methodische Beschreibungen von distinkten Zuständen zu Deskriptionen und Narrationen sozialer Veränderungen, von Übergängen? Und welche neuen Methoden bieten sich im Blick auf diese Fragen durch Big Data? Wie können soziologische Methoden der Erfassung von Transitionen von inter- und transdisziplinären Zugängen profitieren? Ausdrücklich möchten wir an dieser Stelle ermuntern, auch die Methoden und die methodologischen Diskussionen der Nachbardisziplinen mit wahrzunehmen und vorzustellen.

Transitionen als komplexe Untersuchungsgegenstände

Für den Duisburger Soziologiekongress laden wir dazu ein, verschiedenste soziale und gesellschaftliche Phänomene als ›Transitionen‹ zu analysieren, wobei Transitionsphänomene in einer doppelten Hinsicht bestehen: In den Blick kommen Verläufe, Übergänge und Prozesse *als* Untersuchungsgegenstände, aber auch Dynamiken der Veränderung *von* Untersuchungsgegenständen selbst (zu denen auch Begriffe und Konzepte sowie Diskurse zählen). Und nicht zuletzt muss thematisiert werden, wie sich solche Prozesse des Wandels als Übergänge begrifflich und sozialtheoretisch konzeptionieren und empirisch untersuchen lassen.

Aus der Vielzahl möglicher empirischer Phänomene soll im Folgenden nur eines exemplarisch betrachtet werden, an dem deutlich wird, dass Transitionen in ganz verschiedenen Reichweiten und Größenordnungen in enger Verflechtung zu analysieren sind: Die Klimakrise ist ein globales Phänomen, das einerseits selbst als Transition gedacht werden kann, beispielsweise im Sinne sich wandelnder Mensch-Natur-Verhältnisse, veränderter Lebensbedingungen, sich wandelnder Diskurse zu Konsum und Nachhaltigkeit, aber auch in der Analyse des Zustandekommens von klimatischen Ereignissen und ihrer Beeinflussbarkeit.

Andererseits sind die weltweiten wie regionalen Folgen des Klimawandels soziologisch als gesellschaftliche Transitionen deutbar, zum Beispiel indem neue Verständnisse globaler Ausbeutung erarbeitet werden, neue Formen sozialer Ungleichheit oder neue Formen und Modi individueller Differenz entstehen. Daran anschließend lassen sich Konflikte um Ressourcen als Übergang in eine neue geopolitische Ordnung verstehen. Diese sind systematisch verbunden mit auf neue Weise virulenten Fragen von Grenzregimen, von Migration und nationalstaatlichen Lösungsversuchen. Darin verhandelte diskursive Deutungen sind ebenso soziologisch zu beobachten wie die politischen Veränderungen auf geopolitischer, innergesellschaftlicher und familiärer Ebene oder die institutionellen Veränderungen der Wissenschaften, ihrer gesellschaftlichen Relevanzen und Anfechtungen. Es können technische Veränderungen sein, die zu Gesellschaften in Transition führen, oder in (gerade auch soziologischen) Diskursen als solche gedeutet werden. Ebenso wie ausgehend von den Klimatransitionen zahlreiche gesellschaftliche Ebenen in den Blick kommen, die ihrerseits Brüche, Übergänge, Neues aufweisen, wären weitere Prozesse als gesellschaftliche Transitionen auf neue Weise zu denken und zu untersuchen: Ausgehend von politischen Transitionen zum Beispiel die gesellschaftlichen, ökonomischen und auch wissenschaftlichen Dekolonisierungsprozesse – und die Prozesse von (Neo-)Kolonisierungen – oder Transitionen ökonomisch erzeugter Ungleichheiten und damit zusammenhängende Übergänge in Rechtfertigungsordnungen, individuellem Begehren oder administrativen Einhegungen. Zu denken ist auch an die Transitionen von Geschlechterordnungen und die damit zusammenhängenden Veränderungen politischer Zugehörigkeiten und Abgrenzungen, von Identitätskonzepten – und anderes mehr.

Nicht zuletzt stellt sich die Frage, ob und wie die Soziologie an Transitionen teilnimmt, sie fördert oder bremst und auch ihrerseits Transitionen unterliegt. Nicht nur als Beitrag zur Selbstbeschreibung der Gesellschaft spielt die Soziologie eine Rolle für die Auswahl von Problemstellungen und die Form des Problemverständnisses, sondern auch als Akteurin und Moderatorin, die aktiv an Prozessen des Wandels teilnimmt und Deutungen anbietet, die Eingang in den gesellschaftlichen Kommunikationshaushalt finden. Zu untersuchen und zu diskutieren wäre, wo und wie das der Fall ist, sei es in der soziologischen Beratung, in der Begleitung von Bürgerforen oder in der systemischen Gestaltung von Großgruppenprozessen. Die Soziologie kann dank ihres Wissens um die Differenz und Divergenz von Akteursperspektiven eine vermittelnde oder auch zuspitzende Rolle in Transitionen spielen. Wo und wie setzt sie dieses Wissen ein? Wo hat sie ihre eigenen blinden Flecken (soweit sie diese beobachten kann, etwa als kritische Theorie)? Es ist überdies nicht auszuschließen, dass sich die Soziologie im Zuge ihrer Beteiligung an Transitionen auch selbst verändert. Mit ihrem Engagement kann eine objektive Distanz verloren gehen und es können sich methodologische Probleme stellen, die reflektiert werden müssen. So wird die Soziologie selbst zur Akteurin und muss lernen, die Erkenntnisse einer Akteurstheorie auch auf sich selbst anzuwenden. Welche wissenschaftssoziologischen und wissenschaftstheoretischen Schlussfolgerungen sind aber aus einer Entwicklung dieser Art zu ziehen?

Duisburg als Ort des Soziologiekongresses 2025

Wir laden ein nach Duisburg! Die Entwicklung der Stadt Duisburg ist von Aufstiegen, Nieder- und Übergängen geprägt, und wir laden in der Woche des Soziologiekongresses ein, diese Spuren von vergangenen und gegenwärtigen Transitionen in der Stadt zu erkunden und soziologisch zu reflektieren. Duisburg, das ist der »Tatort«-Kommissar Schimanski, ›Wandel durch Kultur – Kultur durch Wandel‹ im Kulturhauptstadtjahr RUHR.2010, die Katastrophe der Love-Parade im selben Jahr, die anhaltende Migration, der größte Binnenhafen Europas, Duisburg als Endstation der Güterzüge aus China auf der ›neuen Seidenstraße‹, aber auch der Wandel von Stadtteilen wie Marxloh von Ausgehmeilen zu Problemvierteln zu Wirtschaftszentren.

Duisburg ist eine Stadt der Transitionen, die von ökologischen Ereignissen beeinflusst wird, in der externe Einflüsse zu internen Transitionen werden und in der soziale, kulturelle und ökologische Transitionen aus sich selbst heraus stattfinden. Der Blick in die Geschichte zeigt, dass Duisburg rund 700 Jahre älter ist als bisher angenommen. Historisch reichen die Spuren nun bis zu den Römern zurück. Im Mittelalter war die Stadt am Rhein ein bedeutendes urbanes Handelszentrum und erlebte eine wirtschaftliche Blütezeit. Duisburg lag am Ende des Hellwegs, zog Kaufleute an und der Handel florierte. Ein Naturereignis beendet diese Phase um 1000 n. Chr. Nach einem starken Hochwasser veränderte sich der Flusslauf. Die Duisburger Rheinschlinge war nun abgetrennt und die Stadt lag landeinwärts, abgeschnitten von der Rheinschifffahrt und den Handelsrouten. Aus der bedeutenden Handelsstadt wurde ein Ackerbürgerstädtchen. Erst im 19. Jahrhundert wurde wieder eine Verbindung zum Rhein geschaffen. Der Hafen wurde ausgebaut und mit den Rohstoffquellen in der Nähe und dem wiedererlangten Zugang zum Rhein als Transportweg gewann Duisburg erneut an Bedeutung.

Nach dem Auf- und Ausbau der Eisen- und Stahlindustrie ab Ende des 19. Jahrhunderts und der Zuwanderung aus vielen Regionen kam es während der Weltwirtschaftskrise zur höchsten Arbeitslosenquote der Weimarer Republik. Der massiven Rüstungsproduktion im Zweiten Weltkrieg folgte die großflächige Zerstörung von Wohngebäuden durch Bombardierungen der Alliierten. Ein weiterer Aufschwung mit Kohle und Stahl brachte Arbeitskräftebedarf, Arbeitsmigration und überdurchschnittliche Wirtschaftskraft. Es folgten jedoch Krise und wirtschaftlicher Niedergang mit der Schließung von Zechen und Hütten, verbunden mit enormen Kaufkraftverlusten und großer Armut spätestens ab den 1970er Jahren. Über ein halbes Jahr hielt der vehemente Widerstand von Stahlwerkern und Stadtgesellschaft gegen die Schließung des Krupp-Stahlwerks in Rheinhausen 1987/88 an. Im Jahr 2008 wurde die letzte Zeche in Duisburg geschlossen. Zugleich ist die Stadt bis heute Standort des größten Stahlwerks Europas, das mit dem Übergang zu ›grüner‹ Technik klimafreundlich werden will. Weltweit erstmalig soll mit dem Duisburger Stadtteil Ruhrort zudem ein urbanes Quartier umweltneutral weiterentwickelt werden.

Auf- und Abstieg lassen sich historisch auch am Beispiel der Universität nachzeichnen. Lange nachdem Gerhard Mercator 1544 in Duisburg Zuflucht gesucht hatte und als angesehener Gelehrter seine Weltkarten schuf, wurde 1655 die »Alte Universität« Duisburg eröffnet, mit einer theologischen, juristischen, medizinischen und philosophischen Fakultät. Duisburg wurde das wissenschaftliche Zentrum des Niederrheins. Ende des 18. Jahrhunderts, das linke Rheinufer war an Frankreich abgetreten, das rechte besetzt, verlor die Universität jedoch Studierende und infolgedessen an Ansehen. 1818 wurde die Universität aufgelöst (Universitätssiegel und große Teile der Bibliothek gingen nach Bonn). 1972 wurde die Gesamthochschule Duisburg neu gegründet (ab 1994 Gerhard-Mercator-Universität), unter anderem mit dem Fach Soziologie. 2003 fusionierten die Duisburger und die Essener Universität-Gesamthochschule zu einer der jüngsten Universitäten in Deutschland.

Die Stadt Duisburg ist damit ein Modell für Wendepunkte und Transitionen, mit tiefgreifenden Auswirkungen für die Stadt und ihre Einwohner:innen. Wie schaut die Soziologie auf diese Transitionen? Wir freuen uns auf anregende Vorträge und lebhafte Diskussionen am Campus Duisburg der UDE!

Stellungnahme der DGS zu Mediendarstellungen von Akademiker:innen im Rahmen politischer Proteste zum Israel-Gaza-Konflikt

Im Rahmen des aktuellen Kriegs Israels in Gaza, der auf den antisemitischen Terror der Hamas vom 7. Oktober 2023 reagiert, finden weltweit und so auch in Deutschland Proteste unter anderem an Universitäten statt. Nachdem in Berlin (wie anderswo) die Proteste Anfang Mai 2024 zum Teil von der Polizei aufgelöst wurden, haben Hunderte Lehrende an (insbesondere Berliner) Universitäten einen offenen Brief unterzeichnet, in dem sie das Vorgehen gegen die (»pro-palästinensischen«) Proteste kritisieren und die Universitätsleitungen dazu aufrufen, auf Dialog statt polizeiliche und juristische Maßnahmen zu setzen. Dieser Brief ist in den Medien sowie der Politik breit und intensiv diskutiert worden – im Sinne einer lebendigen pluralen Demokratie zu Recht. Allerdings hat sich im Anschluss eine regelrechte Medienkampagne entwickelt, die wir als wissenschaftlicher Fachverband inakzeptabel finden. Dagegen wenden wir uns.

Wir verurteilen mit dieser Stellungnahme die mediale Diffamierung und personalisierte, pauschale Verurteilung von Lehrenden, darunter auch Soziolog:innen. Es ist zutiefst beunruhigend, dass in einer aktuellen Kampagne (insbesondere BILD vom 10. Mai 2024) Wissenschaftler:innen – darunter auch jüdische und renommierte Forscher:innen zum Nationalsozialismus, der Shoah und im Bereich des Antisemitismus – durch Massenmedien individuell angeprangert und (ausgerechnet) in Deutschland als »Täter« (sic!) diffamiert werden. Es scheint, dass dabei bestimmte Disziplinen (so auch die Soziologie) und Forschungsfelder (etwa die Postcolonial Studies) als angeblich per se politisch und antisemitisch ins Visier genommen werden. Derartig pauschale, zum Teil klar falsche und diffamierende Darstellungen haben unter Umständen weitreichende forschungspolitische Folgen, vor denen wir warnen. Einer lebendigen politischen Debatte schaden derartige Kampagnen, sie vergiften das Diskussionsklima und haben verheerende Folgen für die Personen, die dabei an den medialen Pranger gestellt werden. Wir halten zudem die Rolle und Aussagen der Wissenschaftsministerin und der Staatssekretärin in diesem Zusammenhang für äußerst bedenklich: Per social media (8. Mai auf der Plattform X) ›Lehrende‹ pauschal in die Nähe des Antisemitismus zu rücken, als gewaltverharmlosend zu bezeichnen und gegenüber der BILD-Zeitung durch Suggestion anzuzweifeln, dass sie »auf dem Boden des Grundgesetzes stehen«, ist politisch mindestens fragwürdig.

Die Deutsche Gesellschaft für Soziologie (DGS) positioniert sich ausdrücklich nicht inhaltlich zu den aktuellen Protesten im Einzelnen und auch nicht zu den Forderungen des offenen Briefes. Die DGS verurteilt klar jeglichen Antisemitismus und jegliche gruppenbezogene Menschenfeindlichkeit; sie wirkt daraufhin, dass auch Hochschulen Orte sind, an denen alle Mitglieder – Studierende, Forschende, administratives und technisches Personal – im rechtlich legitimen Rahmen respektiert und gewaltfrei arbeiten und sich politisch auseinandersetzen können, ohne Diffamierungen oder Bedrohungen befürchten zu müssen.

Prof. Dr. Paula-Irene Villa Braslavsky (Vorsitzende)

Essen, 13. Mai 2024

Aus dem DGS-Vorstand

Liebe Mitglieder der Deutschen Gesellschaft für Soziologie,
der 42. Kongress der DGS wird sich 2025 in Duisburg als Thema mit *Transitionen* auseinandersetzen. *Transitionen* versucht Zwischenräume begrifflich zu fassen. Dabei bilden Offenheit und Kontingenz von Geschichte und Gegenwart den *Erwartungshorizont* (Koselleck) für die Beschreibung solcher Phänomene wie »sozialer *Wandel*, *Transformation*, *Prozess*, *Entwicklung*, *Evolution* oder auch *Revolution*. Mit dem Begriff der ›Transitionen‹ als Leitbegriff für diesen Kongress sollen vor allem die *Verläufe und Dynamiken* gesellschaftlicher, institutioneller wie individueller Veränderungen in ihren unterschiedlichen Qualitäten fokussiert werden«, heißt es im Themenpapier zum Kongress, das Sie hier im Heft ab Seite 328 nachlesen können. Soziale Transitionen konzentrieren sich auf Zustände des *Werdens* und können auf allen Ebenen des Sozialen und in allen Bereichen der Gesellschaft beobachtet und mit vielfältigem Theoriebesteck analysiert werden. Wir freuen uns mit den Kolleg:innen vor Ort schon jetzt auf den lebendigen Fachaustausch in Duisburg!

Mit mindestens ebensolcher Vorfreude sehen wir der kommenden DGS-Konferenz entgegen, die vom 23. bis 25. September in Osnabrück stattfindet. Das Programm ist so gut wie online; es gibt viele verschiedene Formate zum Thema *Klassen – Klassifikationen – Klassifizierungen* (Anmeldung über die DGS Homepage). Die Party wird, wie immer, eine Klasse für sich!

Der 43. Kongress der Deutschen Gesellschaft für Soziologie findet 2026 statt. Ort und Datum sowie das Kongressthema werden auf der DGS-Konferenz in Osnabrück sowie anschließend auf der digitalen Mitgliederversammlung am 26. September bekanntgegeben.

Der DGS-Ausschuss *Partizipation und Barrierefreiheit* ist nun auch auf der Homepage gelistet. Er setzt sich mit bestehenden Barrieren und Partizipationshemmnissen auseinander, die die Teilhabe am fachlichen Austausch in der DGS erschweren können, und entwickelt Vorschläge zur Verbesserung.

Auch die zahlreichen Arbeitskreise in den Sektionen bieten eine gute Übersicht der breiten thematischen Vielfalt des Faches. Der Vorstand überlegt derzeit, wie diese Vielfalt besser zur Geltung kommen kann. Dabei ist der Unterschied zwischen AK und Ausschuss wichtig, da die Ausschüsse durch Konzilsbeschluss eingesetzte Gruppen unter der Leitung eines Vorstandsmitglieds mit einem klaren Arbeitsauftrag sind. Arbeitskreise hingegen werden von den Sektionen initiiert. Wir haben zunächst die Sektionen um Meldung ihrer AKs gebeten. Vielen Dank an die Sektionen!

Bei der Aprilsitzung des Vorstands war der Studentische Beirat dabei. Dieser wird zweimal im Jahr eingeladen, das nächste Mal dann auf der Jahresversammlung am 11. Oktober in Essen. Die Studentin Franca Heuer berichtete von dem Versuch, die studentische Partizipation in der DGS sichtbarer zu machen. Hierzu vernetzt man sich mit der Deutschen Nachwuchsgesellschaft für Politik- und Sozialwissenschaft (DNGPS), die im Sommer eine Tagung in Leipzig organisiert, an der sich auch der Beirat beteiligen wird. Ferner berichtete Sabrina Arneth von einem Treffen mit Studierenden in der DGS und Fachschaftsräten, an dem rund zwanzig Personen teilnahmen. Das Feedback ergab hauptsächlich, dass die Aktivitäten der DGS noch stärker in die Studierendenschaft hinein kommuniziert werden sollten. Grundsätzlich – so der Beirat – soll die ökonomische Situation von Studierenden in Zukunft mehr berücksichtigt werden. Um die Transparenz zu verbessern, wird auf der Homepage ein Wegweiser für Studierende in der DGS erstellt, der auf die Partizipationsmöglichkeit als Beirat, das Fachschaftsticket für den Kongress und andere Vergünstigungen hinweist.

Mit Stellungnahmen machen wir es uns nicht leicht; jede Stellungnahme füttert die toxische Verdachtslogik des ›warum nicht auch zu diesem oder jenem Problem Stellung beziehen‹? Wir gehen zurückhaltend vor, es ist eigentlich nicht Aufgabe des DGS-Vorstands normative oder politische Positionen zu verkünden, die deutlich jenseits der Forschungs- und Hochschulpolitik liegen. Aber manche Vorfälle und Situationen gebieten doch bisweilen ein klares normatives Wort. So etwa bei der Verurteilung des antisemitischen Terrors der Hamas am 7. Oktober 2023, der Betroffenheit über alle Opfer im aktuellen Krieg, und dem Aufruf zur Unterstützung der Kolleg*innen in Israel. Und so auch nun, am 13. Mai 2024, in einer Stellungnahme zur Medienkampagne gegen Lehrende und Forschende im Rahmen der aktuellen Proteste rund um den Krieg in Gaza. Als Fachverband verurteilen wir die mediale Diffamierung und personalisierte, pauschale Verurteilung von Lehrenden, darunter auch Soziolog:innen, wenn diese sich friedlich im Rahmen geltenden Rechts und in ihrer Funktion als Expert:innen zum Thema äußern. Die Stellungnahme finden Sie hier direkt vor diesem Vorstandsbericht auf Seite 338. Wenn Sie sich zur Stellungnahme äußern wollen, ob kritisch, empört, analytisch oder würdigend, oder wenn Sie daran anknüpfend zur Frage, wie wir innerhalb der Disziplin mit Antisemitismus umgehen können, sollen, wollen, etwas schreiben möchten – Gern! Bitte nutzen Sie den SozBlog dazu. Er steht allen offen, eine Email an die Geschäftsstelle genügt.

Ansonsten gilt wie immer: *We'll keep you informed!* Beachten Sie unsere Präsenz in den sozialen Medien, alle wichtigen Infos über Stellenausschreibungen, Neuerscheinungen, Tagungen oder medialen Einlassungen von Soziolog:innen finden Sie auf Mastodon – unter derselben Adresse wie bei X [@DGSoziologie], bei Instagram, facebook und bluesky. Wir nehmen dafür gern Ihre Hinweise entgegen. Auch um die Kommunikationen zwischen den DGS-Sektionen besser zu gestalten, können auf unseren Kanälen die Veranstaltungen der einzelnen Sektionen sehr gut nachverfolgt werden. Natürlich wird die Social Media Präsenz der DGS wie auch unsere Homepage www.soziologie.de stets auf dem neuesten Stand gehalten.

Wenn Sie etwas wissen oder kommentieren möchten, melden Sie sich bei der Geschäftsstelle. Marcel Siepmann (marcel.siepmann@soziologie.de oder marcel.siepmann@kwi-nrw.de, beide Adressen bleiben vorerst gültig) ist Ihr/Euer Ansprechpartner, insbesondere hinsichtlich organisatorischer und verbandsinterner Abläufe. Alle Vorstandsmitglieder sind selbstverständlich auch ansprechbar, Sie finden uns über die Website.

Herzliche Grüße, auch im Namen der Vorstandskolleg:innen,
Paula-Irene Villa Braslavsky

Veränderungen in der Mitgliedschaft

Neue Mitglieder

Dr. phil. Davide Brocchi, Köln
Eva Fabian, Halle (Saale)
Martina Funk, Schwäbisch Gmünd
Clara Heinrich, Berlin
Prof. Dr. Steffen Kohl, Berlin
Daniel Lehnert, M.A., München
Marcel Erik Lemmer, Frankfurt am Main
Kathrin Lutz, Mainz
Eva Reitz, M.A., Mainz
Miriam Schmitt, Wiesbaden
Sabrina Schorr, Bochum
Franziska Zehl, M.A., Würzburg

Neue studentische Mitglieder

Kimberly Schlüter, Mainz
Melanie Wendker, Münster

Austritte

Alexander Brand, B.A., Bamberg
Alexander Brunke, M.A., Berlin
Nadine Brunstein, B.A., Bad Eilsen
Tristan Dohnt, Gießen
Dr. Andreas Göttlich, Konstanz
Dr. Annette Keles, Backnang
Prof. Dr. Andreas Lange, Weingarten
Prof. Dr. Johanna Mierendorff, Halle (Saale)

Dr. Glaucia Peres da Silva, Tübingen
Chiara Porada, Münster
Hannah Marie Schnee, Bremen
Prof. Dr. Wilhelm Schumm, Frankfurt am Main
Dr. Andreas Siegert, Alberstedt
Prof. Dr. Katharina Walgenbach, Hagen

Arbeitskreis Normativitäten

Workshop »›Clash of Normativities‹ – zu einer Soziologie der Erwartungszusammenhänge« am 15. und 16. Februar 2024 in Marburg

Der von *Linda Nell* (Göttingen), *Henning de Vries* (Marburg) und *Marc Mölders* (Mainz) an der Philipps-Universität ausgerichtete Workshop fand als Kooperationsveranstaltung des Arbeitskreises Normativitäten in der Sektion Soziologische Theorie und der Sektion Rechtssoziologie statt. Mit einem Ausblick auf die Themen des Workshops machte Marc Mölders den Auftakt. Er rief in Erinnerung, dass vor dem Hintergrund sich wandelnder politischer und sozialer Verhältnisse neu zu diskutieren sei, ob und wie sich Rechtsnormen beziehungsweise Normativitäten im alltäglichen Leben der ihnen ausgesetzten Subjekte bemerkbar machten und wie unterschiedliche Normerwartungen zusammenhingen.

Panel I nahm die Grundlagen, aber auch die Gefahren für die liberale, demokratische Grundordnung aus soziologischer Perspektive in den Blick. Im Fokus des Panels standen *Clashes* in den Erwartungen der Bürger:innen gegenüber ihren Institutionen beziehungsweise die Ablehnung oder Aneignung von Institutionen und Normen durch bestimmte Gruppen.

Das Panel wurde eröffnet von *Mounir Zahran* (Berlin) mit seinem Vortrag »Erwartungen, Enttäuschungen und Legitimität«. Er besprach, wie sich Erwartungen der Bürger:innen auf die Legitimität von Institutionen und auf die Stabilität eines liberal-demokratischen politischen Systems auswirken. Zentral für das Funktionieren einer liberalen Demokratie sei unter anderem der Schutz der Bürger:innen vor zu großer Enttäuschung ihrer legitimen Erwartungen. Dazu könnten zivilgesellschaftliche Protestkultur, die Aussicht, zukünftig an der Macht beteiligt zu sein, sowie endgültige Entscheidungen von Verfassungsgerichten beitragen. Apathie oder Gewalt könnten hingegen die Folge enttäuschter Erwartungen sein.

Den folgenden Input gestaltete *Johanna Fröhlich* (Basel). Sie befasste sich unter dem Titel »Volk und Person: Zwei unterschiedliche normative Ordnungen?« mit der sogenannten »Neuen Rechten«. Anhand von Beobachtungsprotokollen analysierte Fröhlich deren normative Bezüge auf Gewaltlosigkeit und Meinungsfreiheit, die sich im Diskurs abzeichnen. Diese seien rein strategischer Natur: Die »Neue Rechte« sei gezwungen, sich auf die moderne Verfahrensordnung der Gewaltfreiheit zu beziehen, die die Unterwerfung unter das staatliche Gewaltmonopol und das Verständnis von Individuen mit gleicher Freiheit und Würde postuliere.

Anschließend nahm *Andrea Kretschmann* (Lüneburg) mit den sogenannten Reichsbürger:innen Mitglieder einer antiliberalen, antidemokratischen Szene in den Fokus und stellte unter dem Titel »›Doing Law‹ als Normkollision – Das Beispiel ›Reichsbürger:innen‹« ein aktuelles Forschungsprojekt vor, das den Rechtsgebrauch von Reichsbürger:innen analysiert. Eines der Spezifika der Reichsbürger-Szene liege in der Tatsache, dass sie eine Staatsgründung von unten anstrebe und zu diesem Zweck versuche, entsprechendes Recht zu schaffen. Diese *Doing Law*-Praxis böte Potenzial für Normkollisionen, da ein Rechtspluralismus beispielsweise in Fragen von Ämtern und Gebietsansprüchen nicht möglich sei.

Panel II weitete den Blick auf internationale Konflikte, Gewalt und Recht und wurde mit dem Vortrag »Erwartungszusammenbrüche. Gewalt und Gegengewalt als Irritationsmechanismen« von *Thorsten Benkel* (Passau) eröffnet. Er thematisierte das Verhältnis von Gewalt und Gegengewalt anhand verschiedener Ereignisse, in denen praktizierte (Gegen-)Gewalt moralisch rechtfertigt wurde, da durch jene (Gegen-)Gewalt ein illegitimes, beispielsweise kolonialistisches System angegriffen werde. Es stelle sich vor diesem Hintergrund die Frage, ob Gewalt, die weitere Gewalt unmittelbar unterbinde, einer juristischen Aufarbeitung der Gewalthandlungen vorzuziehen sei. Die internationale Rechtsordnung sei ineffektiv, denn sie könne erstens Gewalt nicht verhindern, werde zweitens von unbeteiligten Dritten getragen, die keine empathische Verbindung zu den Opfern hätten, und agiere drittens ahistorisch.

Auch der folgende Vortrag von *Henning de Vries* bewegte sich auf der Ebene des internationalen Rechts. In seinem Input »Konflikt und Recht im Kontext militärischer Gewalt revisited« stellte er die Frage nach dem Wert des Völkerrechts vor dem Hintergrund aktueller Krisen und Konflikte wie dem Angriffskrieg Russlands gegen die Ukraine. Werde Konflikt als kommunikativer Akt gedacht, gehe es im Konfliktfall auch darum, der gegnerischen Partei die eigene Interpretation der Ereignisse zu verdeutlichen. Recht verkörpere hierbei die Rolle generalisierten normativen Erwartens. Sodann problematisierte de Vries die vor allem im internationalen Konflikt meist uneindeutige Faktenlage, die zur Folge habe, dass die Konfliktparteien in Fragen der Faktendeutung oft weit auseinander liegen.

Panel III verließ die Ebene internationalen Rechts und betrachtete Rechtssysteme in ihrer Wechselwirkung mit anderen gesellschaftlichen Teilordnungen. Den Anfang machte die Soziologin *Linda Nell* mit ihrem Vortrag »Rechtssystem und Rechtssektor – Zur Topographie multipel differenzierter sozialer Ordnungen«. Sie stellte eine Heuristik vor, die von einem Rechtssektor ausgeht, der neben dem Rechtssystem auch rechtsspezifische Organisationen und andere soziale Teilbereiche wie soziale Milieus umfasst und damit neben einer institutionellen auch einer kulturellen Pluralisierung Rechnung trägt. Mit dieser Heuristik lasse sich die Wirkung des Rechts über seine rein funktionale Differenzierung hinaus zeigen. Zudem könne analysiert werden, wie sich unterschiedliche Milieus auf Recht bezögen, entsprechende Praktiken normativ integrierten und dem Rechtssystem so in seiner Funktionserfüllung helfen würden.

Einen weiteren Beitrag zum dritten Panel leistete *Joachim Renn* (Münster) mit einem Input zum Thema »Making it Implicit. Die Radikalisierung abstrakter Normen und die Grundlagen der Demokratie«. Er hob die Bedeutung des affektiven Ethos hervor, das Ausdruck staatsbürgerlicher Normativität sei. Dazu gehöre die Empörung bestimmter, von einem rechtsstaatlichen Ethos geprägter Milieus über verfassungsfeindliche Äußerungen oder Handlungen Einzelner. In diesem Phänomen zeige sich die Verwandlung kognitiv explizierter Normen in implizite, effektive Normativität milieuförmiger Kommunikation. Das Ziel einer solchen Betrachtungsweise sei eine performative Theorie des Verfassungspatriotismus bei multipler Differenzierung.

Den Abschluss bildete der Jurist *Lasse Ramson* (Bremen) mit dem Vortrag »Einheit und Grenzen des Rechtssystems: Bedingungen und Wege der Rekonstruktion«. Er fragte, ob es eine Einheit des Rechtssystems überhaupt gebe und stellte in Frage, dass Rechtspluralismus mittels der Durchsetzung nationalen Rechts bewältigt werden könne. Was als einheitsbildende Modi gelte, beschreibe gleichzeitig die Grenzen des Rechts und zeige, dass Einheit nicht gleichbedeutend sei mit Widerspruchsfreiheit. Die klassischen Wege der Rekonstruktion von Einheit dienten vor allem der Vermeidung von Rechtskollisionen.

Der Workshop bildete ein breites inhaltliches Spektrum ab und folgte dabei einem klaren roten Faden. Im Fokus standen aktuelle gesellschaftliche Themenbereiche wie der Schutz der liberal-demokratischen Grundordnung, die Strategien ihrer Feinde sowie das Konfliktregelungspotenzial des internationalen Rechts. Die Veranstaltung dokumentierte die Relevanz der (Rechts-)Soziologie und trug zur transdisziplinären Vernetzung bei.

Linn-Sophie Löber*

* Mit Dank an Greta Hoffmann und Zeynep Sahin für ihre hilfreichen Mitschriften.

Sektion Frauen- und Geschlechterforschung

Vorstellung der Arbeitsgruppe »Intersektionale Perspektiven auf die Soziologie als disziplinäres Feld«

In Anlehnung an die Schwarze US-amerikanische Soziologin Patricia H. Collins (2019) kann Intersektionalität als »knowledge project« verstanden werden. Dieses ziele nicht nur darauf ab, kritisch-gesellschaftstheoretisches Wissen zu generieren, um die Dynamiken sozialer Ungleichheit und Diskriminierung besser zu verstehen. Vielmehr umfasse Intersektionalität ein breites und widerständiges intellektuelles Projekt, dass kontextabhängig und dialogisch mit (emanzipatorischen) Akteur*innen verschiedener Praxisfelder darüber diskutiert, wie sozialer Wandel im Kontext von Kolonialismus, Nationalismus, Heterosexismus, Rassismus oder neoliberalem Kapitalismus erfolgen kann. Angesichts dringender aktueller sozialer Problemlagen, wie die Zunahme völkisch-autoritärer, extrem-rechter Positionen und von rassistischer, antisemitischer, sexualisierter und transfeindlicher Gewalt sowie die gewaltvollen Folgen neokolonialer und planetarischer Zerstörung, halten wir diese gesellschaftskritische Fundierung des intersektionalen Projektes für richtungsweisend. Ähnlich hielt auch die Themenbeschreibung des 41. Kongress der Deutschen Gesellschaft für Soziologie, auf dem sich diese AG gründete, fest, dass sich gegenwärtig »[a]bhängig von Kontinent, Region aber auch Klasse oder Geschlecht […] bereits bestehende Ungleichheiten wie Polarisierungen zu verschärfen« scheinen (o.A. 2021: 495).

Standortbestimmung

Als im Laufe des frühen 21. Jahrhunderts Intersektionalität allmählich Eingang fand in die deutsche Frauen- und Geschlechterforschung, stießen Konzept und Begriff zwar bei einigen auf große Zustimmung, insbesondere bei den Pionierinnen der Schwarzen Frauenbewegung (s.u.), gleichzeitig wurde Skepsis gegenüber diesem ›US-Import‹ laut: So stellte beispielsweise Bührmann (2009: 31) die Paradigmafrage und resümierte, dass eine Pioniergeschichte sowie ein Gründungsnarrativ fehlen und ein »Mangel an glaubwürdigen Quellen« bestehe. Dagegen haben Lutz, Herrera Vivar und Supik (2013: 12) eingewendet, dass soziale Bewegungen und Theorien im internationalen Austausch erörtert werden und in Deutschland vor allem Schwarze

Sozialwissenschaftler*innen die Anglo-Amerikanische Debatte als sehr hilfreich empfanden, um damit das Phänomen des deutschen Rassismus, das nach dem Zweiten Weltkrieg in den Sozialwissenschaften stark tabuisiert wurde, zu erforschen (siehe Lutz 2013: 421 ff.). Darüber hinaus seien die von Walgenbach (2007) formulierten ›vielfältige[n] Genealogien‹ auch in der hiesigen Debatte relevant.

In der deutschsprachigen soziologisch-feministischen Debatte war die Erörterung des Ineinandergreifens und der Wechselwirkungen kategorialer Ungleichheiten und komplexer Benachteiligungsprozesse lange Zeit vorrangig in Bezug auf Klassenverhältnisse im Kapitalismus erfolgt (siehe unter anderem Beer 1989, Gottschall 2000). Dazu gab es primär aus der Perspektive lesbischer Feministinnen Kritik an der Vernachlässigung der Kategorie Sexualität, als auch an der Tatsache, dass ›Disability‹ (körperliche Einschränkungen/Behinderungen) als Kategorie sozialer Benachteiligung unbeachtet blieb (Waldschmidt 2003). Impulse, diese Debatten zu erweitern um die notwendige Auseinandersetzung über Differenzen zwischen Frauen, und hier insbesondere um die Kategorie ›Rassismus‹, gab es bereits seit den 1980er Jahren. Ein Beispiel dafür sind die dokumentierten Äußerungen von Wut und Ärger eingewanderter Frauen beim ›Ersten gemeinsamen Kongress ausländischer und deutscher Frauen‹ im März 1984 in Frankfurt, die ihren ›Schwestern‹ vorwarfen, paternalistisch und rassistisch zu sein, sich weder mit den Diskriminierungen der deutschen Ausländergesetzgebung, noch mit den vielfältigen alltäglichen Ausgrenzungen Schwarzer Deutscher und ›ausländischer Frauen‹ zu beschäftigen.

Intersektionale Dynamiken im Feld der Soziologie

Die AG »Intersektionale Perspektiven auf die Soziologie als disziplinäres Feld« ist aus der Ad-hoc Gruppe »Gesellschaftliche Polarisierungen in der Soziologie? Intersektionale Perspektiven in der Soziologie« auf dem DGS-Kongress 2022 hervorgegangen. Sie setzt sich aus Mitgliedern der Sektionen Frauen- und Geschlechterforschung, Biografieforschung, Soziologiegeschichte sowie Migration und ethnische Minderheiten zusammen. Dieser Zusammenschluss möchte Voraussetzungen schaffen, um Ungleichheitsprozesse und Benachteiligungsstrukturen innerhalb der Soziologie aus einer intersektionalen Perspektive zu untersuchen. Bislang fehlt eine systematische intersektionale Analyse von Zugangschancen, Mechanismen von Marginalisierung und Ausschlüssen im deutschsprachigen soziologischen Feld unter Berücksichtigung von Geschlecht/Gender, Ethnisierungs- und Rassifizierungsprozessen, sozialer Herkunft und weiteren sozialen Kategorien und Differenzierungen.

Der kritische Blick ins Außen, der nach den flexibilisierten sowie beständigen Mechanismen der Differenz/Ungleichheit in der Gesellschaft sucht, muss dem Anspruch der Reflexivität folgen und untersuchen, wie intersektionale Marginalisierungs- und Ausschlussdynamiken im (eigenen) Feld der Soziologie virulent waren und sind. Zwar haben Instrumente der Gleichstellung und Anti-Diskriminierung seit den 1980er Jahren erste Effekte gezeitigt und einigen Wissenschaftlerinnen den Weg in die soziologische Karriere geebnet. Allerdings sind die bisherigen Gleichstellungsinstrumente eher eindimensional – entlang der Dimensionen Geschlecht – beleuchtet und praktiziert worden. Sie sind als weiche Einflussmöglichkeiten zu verstehen und weisen Akteursabhängigkeiten auf. Auch werden neue Formen der Diskriminierungen sichtbar (zum Beispiel von non-binären Personen, nicht-*weißen*, rassifizierten und migrantisierten Personen).

Aus diesen Gründen plädieren wir für eine Erhebung, die mit einer intersektionalen Perspektive auf die Ein- und Ausschlüsse in der Soziologie schaut und einen datenbasierten Ist-Zustand zeigt: Welche Diskriminierungsformen werden auf der Ebene der Wissensproduktion sichtbar (zum Beispiel durch Zitierpraktiken oder Diskussionen um Wissenschaftsfreiheit)? Wie werden Ungleichheitsmechanismen durch soziale Praktiken (zum Beispiel Einstellungspraktiken oder Drittmittelvergabe) (re)produziert? Welche Zuschreibungen, Subjektivierungsweisen und Identitätspolitiken führen zu Ausschlüssen, welche wiederum gelten als unmarkiert/akzeptiert und gehen mit Privilegierungen im soziologischen Feld einher (zum Beispiel wer beginnt ein Soziologiestudium, wer verlässt die universitäre Laufbahn nach der Promotion, wer wird auf eine Professur berufen)? Wer gilt als passfähig? Welche Laufbahnen von Soziolog*innen lassen sich rekonstruieren und inwiefern hängen sie mit der Zugehörigkeit zu einer sozialen Gruppe zusammen?

Mitglieder der AG sind Anna Amelina, Jördis Grabow, Barbara Grüning, Encarnación Gutiérrez Rodríguez, Ingrid Jungwirth, Helma Lutz, Minna-Kristiina Ruokonen-Engler und Miriam Friz Trzeciak.

Jördis Grabow, Helma Lutz, Miriam Friz Trzeciak

Literatur

Beer, Ursula 1989 (Hg.): Klasse Geschlecht. Feministische Gesellschaftsanalyse und Wissenschaftskritik. Bielefeld: AJZ Verlag.

Bührmann, Andrea 2009: Intersectionality – ein Forschungsfeld auf dem Weg zum Paradigma? Tendenzen, Herausforderungen und Perspektiven der Forschung über Intersektionalität. Gender. Zeitschrift für Geschlecht, Kultur und Gesellschaft, 1. Jg., Heft 2, 28–44.

Gottschall, Karin 2000: Soziale Ungleichheit und Geschlecht. Kontinuitäten und Brüche, Sackgassen und Erkenntnispotentiale im deutschen soziologischen Diskurs. Opladen: Leske und Budrich.

Hill Collins, Patricia 2019: Intersectionality as Critical Social Theory. Durham, London: Duke University Press.

Lutz, Helma 2013: ›Intersectional invisibility‹ – Über das Auftauchen und Verschwinden von Kategorien sozialer Ungleichheit in der deutschen Intersektionalitätsdebatte. Erwägen Wissen Ethik, Forum für Erwägungskultur, 24. Jg., Heft 3, 421–423.

Lutz, Helma / Herrera Vivar, Maria Teresa / Supik, Linda 2013: Fokus Intersektionalität – eine Einleitung. In Helma Lutz / Maria Teresa Herrera Vivar / Linda Supik (Hg.), Fokus Intersektionalität. Bewegungen und Verortungen eines vielschichtigen Konzeptes. Wiesbaden: Springer VS, 9–31.

o.A. 2021: Polarisierte Welten. Themenpapier zum 41. Kongress der Deutschen Gesellschaft für Soziologie vom 26. bis 30. September 2022 in Bielefeld. SOZIOLOGIE, 50. Jg., Heft 4, 495–502. https://kongress2022.soziologie.de thema.

Waldschmidt, Anne 2003 (Hg): Kulturwissenschaftliche Perspektiven der Disability Studies. Tagungsdokumentation. Schriftenreihe zum selbstbestimmten Leben Behinderter. Kassel: Bifos.

Walgenbach, Katharina 2007: Gender als interdependente Kategorie. In Katharina Walgenbach / Gabriele Dietze / Lann Hornscheidt / Kerstin Palm (Hg.), Gender als interdependente Kategorie: neue Perspektiven auf Intersektionalität, Diversität und Heterogenität. Opladen: Barbara Budrich, 23–64.

Sektion Methoden der qualitativen Sozialforschung

Frühjahrstagung »Schreiben – Forschen – Publizieren. Textproduktion in der qualitativen Sozialforschung« am 14. und 15. März 2024 am Kulturwissenschaftlichen Institut Essen

Die Tagung der Sektion Methoden der qualitativen Sozialforschung wurde stellvertretend für das DFG-Netzwerk »Textuelle Performanz in der qualitativen Sozialforschung« von Oliver Berli, Judith Eckert, Hannes Krämer, Björn Krey und Vivien Sommer organisiert.

Die Soziologie ist eine schreibende Wissenschaft, dies gilt umso mehr in der qualitativen Sozialforschung. Im Schreiben manifestiert sich ein Ineinandergreifen von Theorie und Empirie, das sich nicht erst in der fertigen Publikation für die Fachcommunity niederschlägt. Obwohl das Schreiben ein zentraler Bestandteil soziologischen Denkens und Forschens ist, sind die Praktiken, die Publikations- und Lehrbedingungen als auch die Qualität des Schreibens in der qualitativen Sozialforschung kaum Gegenstand einer theoretischen sowie empirischen Reflexion. In den elf Vorträgen der drei Themenfelder der Tagung *Schreibtraditionen*, *Publikationsbedingungen/-formate* und *Schreibdidaktik* gelang es, die Textproduktion in der qualitativen Sozialforschung aus einer Vielzahl an Perspektiven zu reflektieren und zu diskutieren.

Den thematischen Einstieg gab *Michaela Pfadenhauer* (Wien), die den Blick auf das *Schreiben in der (lebensweltanalytischen) Ethnographie* lenkte. In ihrem Vortrag reflektierte sie die Praxis ethnographischen Schreibens als eine des Praxis-Beschreibens, durch das das Selbstverständliche, Implizite und Stumme des menschlichen Zusammenlebens zur Sprache gebracht wird und außerdem zwischen Sinnwelten »übersetzt« werden muss. Wissenschaftliches Lesen und Schreiben, so betonte sie, sind Praktiken der wissenschaftlichen Wissensherstellung, die es zu reflektieren gelte.

Im zweiten Vortrag widmete sich *Tim Seitz* (Frankfurt am Main) dem Zusammenhang zwischen *Schreiben und Zeichnen*. Er reflektierte anhand seiner eigenen Forschungspraxis die wichtige Rolle, die Zeichnungen als epistemische Praktik in der qualitativen Sozialforschung spielen, der jedoch bisher zu wenig Aufmerksamkeit geschenkt werde – und deren Verhältnis zum Schreiben weiter auszuloten sei.

Inga-Marie Schröer (Berlin) setzte sich in ihrem Vortrag mit *Schreibprozessen in qualitativen Doktorarbeiten* auseinander. Mit ihrer Analyse zeigt sie das Spannungsfeld zwischen der notwendigen Struktur und dem nötigen Freiraum zum Schreiben, insbesondere vor dem Hintergrund des Publikationsdrucks.

In Gemeinschaft zu schreiben, kann zur Strukturierung und Motivation genutzt werden, und so wächst der Markt von Online-Schreibcommunities hin zum Streaming vom eigenen Schreibtisch aus.

Ajit Singh (Bielefeld) lenkte den Blick auf die Herausforderung, *technologisch mediatisierte Wissens-* sowie *Kommunikationskulturen* zu beforschen: Das technisierte Fachwissen eines Feldes müssen Forschende erst interpretativ aufbrechen sowie »übersetzen«, um es zugänglich zu machen. In seinem Fazit hob er die Schwierigkeiten hervor, Unsichtbarkeiten in technisch vermittelten Handlungen sowie die Schweigsamkeit technologischer Abläufe (schriftlich) zu rekonstruieren.

Yves Jeanrenaud (München) setzte sich in seinem Vortrag mit den *Folgen von KI für die qualitative Sozialforschung* auseinander. Er präsentierte forschungspraktische und -ethische Fragen im Umgang mit der KI im Zusammenhang mit Transkription von Interviews und in der qualitativen Auswertung von Daten.

Anschließend berichtete *Lars Alberth* (Lüneburg) über seine didaktischen Erfahrungen in einem *Schreibseminar mit Masterstudierenden.* Er analysiert sein Schreibseminar als »ungewolltes ethnomethodologisches Krisenexperiment«, denn die Drop-Out-Rate sei sehr hoch. Die Seminargestaltung mit ihrer eigenen sozialen Organisation von Arbeitsaufträgen, Rechten und Rechenschaftspflichten kollidierte mit der bisherigen (Schreib-)Praxis der studentischen Autonomie. Zugleich fiel es den Studierenden schwer, Texte zu teilen, Feedback zu geben und anzunehmen. Die rege Diskussion verdeutlichte, dass Seminare zum Schreiben in der Soziologie nach wie vor rar sind.

Nathalie-Ann Köbli und *Cornelia Schadler* (beide Wien) präsentierten in ihrem Vortrag *Publishing als Game* – auch stellvertretend für ihre Co-Autor:innen Luisa Leisenheimer und Mira Achter – erste Ergebnisse aus ihrem Projekt »Entangled Publications« zu sich verändernden Publikationspraktiken. Für die meisten Wissenschaftsdisziplinen lasse sich ein Wechsel von Monographien hin zu Journalbeiträgen feststellen, während zugleich der Publikationsdruck zunehme. Gleichzeitig werden immer mehr wissenschaftliche Arbeiten auf Englisch publiziert. In der Folge publizieren nicht-US-amerikanische Wissenschaftler:innen für verschiedene Communities, um lokal und universell lesbar zu sein – eine immense Mehrfachbelastung.

Laura Behrmann (Wuppertal) und *Oliver Berli* (Ludwigsburg), Leiter:innen des DFG-Netzwerks, stellten ihre Forschungsergebnisse zur *textuellen Performanz in der qualitativen Sozialforschung in Deutschland und den USA* vor. Während deutschsprachige soziologische Artikel stärker auf die theoretischen und methodologischen Prämissen einer Forschungsarbeit eingehen, lehnen sich US-amerikanische qualitative Artikel an die Sprach- und Begründungslogik der quantitativen Sozialforschung an, weisen aber zugleich eine stärkere Narrativität auf als ihre deutschen Pendants. Der Vortrag macht deutlich, dass es sich lohnt, Repräsentationsformen und das Verhältnis von Wissenskulturen und Schreibpraktiken weiter zu erforschen.

Den Abschluss bildete die closing lecture von *Annette Lareau* (Pennsylvania), die in ihrem Vortrag Dos and Don'ts hinsichtlich des Publizierens im englischsprachigen Raum in Bezug auf die Aspekte *Klarheit, Evidenz und Argumentation* herausarbeitete, Einblick in die Herausforderungen des Schreiben gab und einige Umgangsstrategien teilte. Sie stellte die »so what?«-Frage, die darauf zielt, den konzeptuellen Beitrag der jeweiligen Studie beziehungsweise Publikation zu klären und das zugrundeliegende empirische Vorhaben an relevante Fachdebatten anzubinden. Sie präsentiert als zentrale Strategie des Überzeugens: »Show the reader (rather than telling the reader)«. Unterstützend verwies Lareau auf Schreibgruppen, in denen sich Forschende regelmäßig treffen, um individuelle Schreibziele zu fixieren und Textentwürfe der Mitglieder zu kommentieren.

Insgesamt war die Tagung geprägt von einem tiefgreifenden und lebhaften Austausch über die Praktiken, Potenziale sowie Herausforderungen des Schreibens in der qualitativen Sozialforschung – auch über Deutschland hinaus. Die Vorträge boten einen facettenreichen Einblick in die vielschichtigen Aspekte der Textproduktion. Es wurde deutlich, dass das Schreiben nicht nur ein Mittel zur Kommunikation von Forschungsergebnissen ist, sondern auch ein zentraler Bestandteil des Forschungsprozesses und soziologischen Denkens selbst, der eng mit der epistemologischen und methodologischen Ausbildung von Forschenden verbunden ist. Die vielfältige Diskussionen verdeutlichten den Bedarf, die Formen und Güte des Schreibens in der (qualitativen) Sozialforschung weiter zu erforschen und zu reflektieren, auch vor dem Hintergrund von KI und erhöhtem Publikationsdruck.

Kristina Schäfer

Der Rat für Sozial- und Wirtschaftsdaten: Ziele – Bedeutung – Tätigkeitsfelder

Alle drei Jahre nominieren die Fachgesellschaften der sozial-, bildungs-, verhaltens- und wirtwissenschaftlichen Disziplinen Kandidat:innen für die Wahl in den Rat für Sozial- und Wirtschaftsdaten (kurz: RatSWD), die dann durch die Wissenschaftsgemeinschaft gewählt werden können. Dies geschah zum letzten Mal im März des vergangenen Jahres, als wir beide durch die DGS nominiert, gewählt und zum 1. Juli 2023 für drei Jahre in den RatSWD berufen wurden. Dies nehmen wir zum Anlass, über dieses Gremium zu informieren und aus seiner vergangenen und aktuellen Arbeit zu berichten.

Was ist der RatSWD und was will er?

Der Rat für Sozial- und Wirtschaftsdaten ist ein unabhängiger Beirat der Bundesregierung, der die Bundes- und Landespolitik zu Fragen der Forschungsinfrastruktur berät. Er besteht aus zehn gewählten Vertreter:innen der empirischen Sozialforschung und zehn Vertreter:innen der wichtigsten Einrichtungen der Datenproduktion in Deutschland, die qua Amt eingesetzt werden. Finanziert wird die Arbeit des Rates durch die DFG, unterstützt wird sie von einer Geschäftsstelle, die am WZB in Berlin angesiedelt ist.

Das wichtigste Ziel der Arbeit des RatSWD besteht bis heute darin, die Basis und den Zugang der empirischen Sozialwissenschaften zu qualitativ hochwertigen, wissenschaftlich relevanten Daten aus administrativen, wissenschaftlichen oder privatwirtschaftlichen Quellen zu verbessern. Dazu entwirft der RatSWD Empfehlungen, berät die für Forschung zuständigen Ministerien, unterstützt und berät Gesetzgebungsverfahren, monitort aktuelle rechtliche, methodische und technologische Entwicklungen und beteiligt sich an Initiativen und Abstimmungen mit internationalen Akteuren. Der RatSWD bildet außerdem ein zentrales Forum für den Austausch und Dialog zwischen der Wissenschaftsgemeinschaft und der Datenproduktion und organisiert alle drei Jahre die Konferenz für Sozial- und Wirtschaftsdaten (KSWD), um wissenschaftliche Themen im Kontext von empirischer Sozialforschung und der Datenproduktion zu diskutieren und Öffentlichkeit dafür zu generieren.

Anfänge und Entwicklungen

Ende der 1990er Jahre veröffentlichten drei einflussreiche Wirtschaftsforscher ein Memorandum, in dem sie den unzureichenden Datenzugang der empirischen Wirtschafts- und Sozialforschung bemängelten und Vorschläge zur Verbesserung der Dateninfrastruktur machten. Zu dieser Zeit gab es kaum Einflussmöglichkeiten der Wissenschaft auf die Generierung amtlicher Umfragedaten, es gab noch keine Forschungsdatenzentren und mithin kaum Transparenz über Datenquellen, und viele Datenbestände waren für die Wissenschaft nicht zugänglich, weil die Daten nicht entsprechend aufbereitet, anonymisiert und dokumentiert waren. Als Reaktion darauf berief das BMBF die »Kommission zur Verbesserung der informationellen Infrastruktur zwischen Wissenschaft und Statistik« (KVI) ins Leben, die im Jahr 2001 ein Gutachten erstellte, in dem eine Reihe von Maßnahmen zur Verbesserung der Dateninfrastruktur beschrieben wurde. Dort wurde auch die Einrichtung eines Rates für Sozial- und Wirtschaftsdaten vorgeschlagen, um den Ausbau der Dateninfrastruktur zu begleiten. Ebenfalls im Jahr 2001 berief das BMBF einen Gründungsausschuss unter dem Vorsitz von Karl-Ulrich Mayer, und im Jahr 2004 nahm der RatSWD unter dem Vorsitz von Gert G. Wagner dann seine Arbeit auf.

Seit 2020 haben die Arbeiten des RatSWD durch die Initiative zum Aufbau einer nationalen Forschungsdateninfrastruktur (NFDI) enorm an Bedeutung gewonnen. Zur NDFI gehören 26 Konsortien aus ganz unterschiedlichen Disziplinen, darunter auch das Konsortium für die Sozial-, Bildungs-, Verhaltens- und Wirtschaftswissenschaften KonsortSWD, das sich dem Auf- und Ausbau der Infrastruktur sozialwissenschaftlicher Daten widmet und die Arbeit mit Daten für die Forschung erleichtern will.[1] Dabei werden die Bedürfnisse der Forschungscommunities sowie rechtliche und ethische Anforderungen berücksichtigt. Seitdem ist der RatSWD ein Teil von KonsortSWD.

1 www.konsort swd.de

Themen und Ergebnisse

Die Anfangsjahre des RatSWD waren vor allem dadurch geprägt, dass die ersten Forschungsdatenzentren eingerichtet wurden, die einen geregelten, transparenten und für alle Wissenschaftler:innen offenen Zugang insbesondere zu sensiblen Daten ermöglichten. Der Datenzugang für die Wissenschaft wurde damit stark verbessert und erweitert. Seitdem sind Entscheidungen über die Akkreditierung neuer Forschungsdatenzentren eine wichtige Daueraufgabe des Rates, und mittlerweile gibt es 41 akkreditierte Forschungsdatenzentren in Deutschland.[2] In diesem Zusammenhang hat auch das Thema Datenerschließung und Forschungsdatenmanagement, insbesondere die Umsetzung der sogenannten FAIR-Prinzipien – Daten sollen auffindbar, zugänglich, interoperabel und nachnutzbar sein – den RatSWD in seiner Arbeit immer wieder begleitet. In den letzten Jahren hat sich der Rat dabei verstärkt dem Management qualitativer Daten sowie dem Datenmanagement in kleinen Forschungsprojekten gewidmet.

Daneben ist die Verbesserung des Zugangs zu Forschungsdaten das wichtigste Thema der Arbeit des Rates. Hier wurde einiges erreicht, aber es gibt immer noch viele ungenutzte Möglichkeiten. In früheren Berufungsperioden setzte sich der Rat mit der Kriminalstatistik, mit Geo-, Migrations- und Bildungsdaten, Big Data und dem technischen Datenzugang (vor allem mit Remote Access) auseinander. Diese Themen berühren fast immer Fragen des Datenschutzes bei Forschungsdaten, so dass sich der Rat auch damit intensiv beschäftigt hat und über die Jahre eine Vorreiterrolle bei der Etablierung und Konsolidierung von Standards eingenommen hat. Dabei greift der Rat die wachsenden technischen und rechtlichen Herausforderungen in Deutschland und Europa kontinuierlich auf, um auch künftig eine Infrastruktur zu ermöglichen, die die datenschutzkonforme Bereitstellung von Forschungsdaten für die Wissenschaft ermöglicht. Eng damit verknüpft sind Fragen der Forschungsethik, denn auch wenn Forschungsaktivitäten rechtlich zulässig sind, müssen sie ethisch nicht zwangsläufig immer vertretbar sein. Forschungsethische Probleme werden zunehmend auch in den Sozialwissenschaften thematisiert, und Fördergeber, wie die DFG oder Fachzeitschriften, verlangen immer häufiger die Klärung der Unbedenklichkeit von Forschungsvorhaben durch Ethikkommissionen, insbesondere wenn Daten erhoben werden sollen. Auch mit diesem Thema hat sich der RatSWD beschäftigt, zum Beispiel mit mehreren Arbeitsgruppen zur Forschungsethik.

2 Für eine Übersicht vgl. www.konsortswd.de/angebote/forschende/alle-datenzentren/

Über die Jahre hat der RatSWD zu allen diesen Bereichen eine Vielzahl von Best-Practice-Sammlungen, Materialien für die akademische Lehre, Handreichungen, Stellungnahmen und Empfehlungen erarbeitet und etliche Beiträge in seiner Working Paper Reihe zu diesen und weiteren Themen veröffentlicht. All diese wertvollen Informationsquellen sind online auf der Webseite des Rates verfügbar.[3]

Wie arbeitet der RatSWD und was tun wir aktuell?

Der RatSWD als Ganzes trifft sich mehrmals im Jahr zu Arbeitssitzungen. Das Gros der Arbeit findet aber in den Arbeitsgruppen und Task Forces statt, die zu Beginn jeder Berufungsperiode in einem Arbeitsprogramm (vgl. dazu aktuell RatSWD 2024) festgelegt, arbeitsteilig besetzt werden und die sich ebenfalls mehrmals im Jahr treffen. In der aktuellen 8. Berufungsperiode gibt es insgesamt fünf Arbeitsgruppen: Eine AG beschäftigt sich mit Datentreuhandmodellen, die es ermöglichen, die Zusammenführung von Datenbeständen über unterschiedliche Anbieter und Produzenten hinweg für Forschungszwecke zu ermöglichen. Eine AG widmet sich den Potenzialen und der Verbesserung von Zugängen zu Gesundheitsdaten. Eine AG hat zum Ziel, ein Infrastrukturangebot zu entwickeln, das es ermöglicht, Vulnerabilitäten, Resilienz und Bereitschaft in Krisen, Katastrophen und Bedrohungslagen aus sozialwissenschaftlicher Perspektive zu untersuchen. Eine AG zielt darauf ab, Unternehmensdaten zu erschließen und besser für die Forschung nutzbar zu machen. Und eine AG widmet sich der Aufgabe, die vielfältigen Daten, die aus der Arbeit von Parlamenten anfallen, in den Blick zu nehmen, um ihre Zugänglichkeit und Strukturierung zu verbessern.

Neben den Arbeitsgruppen gibt es aktuell drei Task Forces, die dauerhaft eingerichtet sind und anlassbezogen tätig werden: Die Task Force Politik und Recht analysiert einschlägige Gesetzentwürfe, erarbeitet Stellungnahmen an die Politik und entwickelt proaktiv Empfehlungen zu relevanten Feldern. Die Task Force Ethik arbeitet an einer dauerhaften Lösung für die Information und Koordination von Ethikkommissionen in den Disziplinen, die im RatSWD vertreten sind. Und schließlich wirft die Task Force Internationales den Blick über den deutschen Tellerrand hinaus auf den Ausbau

3 www.konsortswd.de/ueber-uns/ratswd/

der europäischen Dateninfrastruktur und auf Best Practices in anderen Ländern. Sie beobachtet die europäische Datengesetzgebung und vernetzt sich international.

Zurzeit arbeiten wir, Corinna Kleinert und Hubert Knoblauch, als die beiden von der DGS (im Falle von Corinna Kleinert gemeinsam mit der Akademie für Soziologie) nominierten Mitglieder, im RatSWD als Ganzem sowie in jeweils drei Arbeitsgruppen beziehungsweise Taskforces. Wir versuchen dabei, die Interessen der soziologischen Forschungscommunities zu vertreten, die Daten erheben, verarbeiten, verwalten und (auch sekundär) nutzen, und zwar sowohl der quantitativen wie auch der neuerdings ebenso präsenten qualitativen Daten. Wir stehen dazu in Kontakt mit dem Vorstand der DGS, haben aber auch ein offenes Ohr für Nachfragen, Anregungen und Kommentare der Mitglieder der DGS.

Corinna Kleinert
E-Mail: corinna.kleinert@lifbi.de und

Hubert Knoblauch
E-Mail: Hubert.Knoblauch@tu-berlin.de

Referenzen

RatSWD – Rat für Sozial- und Wirtschaftsdaten 2024: Arbeitsprogramm der 8. Berufungsperiode 2023–2026. Berlin. https://doi.org/10.17620/02671.93

Klaus-Mehnert-Preis

Die Deutsche Gesellschaft für Osteuropakunde vergibt jährlich den Klaus-Mehnert-Preis zur Förderung junger Wissenschaftlerinnen und Wissenschaftler. Ausgezeichnet werden herausragende wissenschaftliche Arbeiten Dissertationen, die sich mit den Staaten Ostmittel- und Osteuropas befassen. Die Arbeiten sollen im deutschsprachigen Bereich verfasst (die Einreichung von Arbeiten, die in englischer Sprache verfasst sind, ist möglich) und zum Zeitpunkt der Bewerbung nicht älter als zwei Jahre sein. Das Verfahren (Verteidigung) muss zum Zeitpunkt der Bewerbung abgeschlossen sein. Hochschullehrerinnen und -lehrer können (im Einverständnis mit der Verfasserin bzw. dem Verfasser) Personen für die Preisverleihung vorschlagen. Interessierte Personen können sich mit ihrer Arbeit aber auch direkt bewerben. Die Förderung erfolgt unabhängig von einer Mitgliedschaft bei der Deutschen Gesellschaft für Osteuropakunde. Das Preisgeld wird seit dem Jahr 2015 von der Klaus-Mehnert-Gedächtnis-Stiftung bereitgestellt. Bitte senden Sie uns zunächst eine formlose E-Mail mit folgenden Angaben.

- Name und Adresse der/des Verfasser*in
- Titel der Arbeit
- Zeitpunkt und Ort der Einreichung (Hochschule und Fakultät)
- Zusammenfassung der Arbeit (max. 2 Seiten) als Anhang

In einem zweiten Schritt werden wir Sie um die Einreichung Ihrer vollständigen Unterlagen in digitaler Form bitten

- die wissenschaftliche Arbeit
- das Erst- und Zweitgutachten
- einen Lebenslauf

Einsendeschluss ist der **1. Oktober 2024**. Weitere Informationen zum Preis finden Sie unter: http://www.dgo-online. org/klaus-mehnert-preis/.

Kontakt:
Dr. Gabriele Freitag
Deutsche Gesellschaft für Osteuropakunde e.V.
Schaperstraße 30
D-10719 Berlin
Tel.: +49(0)30 214 784 12
E-Mail: info@dgo-online.org

Habilitationen

Dr. Lisa Suckert hat sich am 9. April 2024 an der Universität Hamburg habilitiert. Die Habilitationsschrift trägt den Titel »Krisenzeiten: Wirtschaftssoziologische Perspektiven auf Zeitlichkeit, Zeithorizonte und Zukunftsvorstellungen im Kontext gesellschaftlicher Krisen«. Die venia legendi lautet Soziologie.

Dr. Insa Pruisken hat sich am 31. Januar 2024 an der Universität Bremen habilitiert. Die Habilitationsschrift trägt den Titel »Institutionelle Logiken, religiöse Organisation und Marktbildung«. Die venia legendi lautet Soziologie.

Dr. Alban Knecht hat sich am 10. Januar 2024 an der Bergischen Universität Wuppertal habilitiert. Die Habilitationsschrift trägt den Titel »Soziale Arbeit im Wandel des Wohlfahrtsstaats«. Die venia legendi lautet Sozialpädagogik und Sozialpolitik.

Dr. Uta Karstein hat sich am 15. November 2023 an der Technischen Universität Dresden habilitiert. Die Habilitationsschrift trägt den Titel »Religion im 19. Jahrhundert. Ästhetik – Öffentlichkeit – Autonomie«. Die venia legendi lautet Soziologie.

Call for Papers

Die Vielfalt des Rechts

Themenoffene Tagung der Sektion Rechtssoziologie am 12. und 13. Dezember 2024 in Marburg

Die Auseinandersetzungen um das Recht sind vielfältig: Der russische Angriffskrieg auf die Ukraine, die Situation im Nahen Osten seit dem Überfall der Hamas auf Israel, die anhaltende Debatte über Flucht und Migration, die Umsturzpläne der Reichsbürger:innenbewegung um Prinz Reuß, das in Bayern beschlossene Verbot des Genderns in öffentlichen Einrichtungen oder die Transformation zu Klimaneutralität am Beispiel des Heizungsgesetzes zeigen, wie prekär, umstritten, politisch sowie gesellschaftlich relevant und – in Anlehnung an Eugen Ehrlich – lebendig Recht sein kann.

In Anbetracht der vielfältigen Themen der Rechtssoziologie, aber auch angesichts unterschiedlicher theoretischer wie methodischer Herangehensweisen lädt der Vorstand der Sektion Rechtssoziologie zu einer offenen Tagung am 12. und 13. Dezember an der Philipps-Universität Marburg ein. Sie bietet ein theorie-, methoden- und themenunabhängiges Forum, um aktuelle Projekte zu präsentieren, grundlegende Fragen zur Debatte zu stellen und in Diskussion miteinander zu treten.

Für die Tagung bitten wir um Zusendung aussagekräftiger Abstracts bis zum **31. August 2024**.

- Einzelvorträge: 500 Wörter
- gemeinsame Panel: 800 Wörter
- weitere Gestaltungsideen wie Author-meets-Critics, Diskussionsrunden usw. werden explizit begrüßt: 800 Wörter

Darüber hinaus rufen wir zur Einreichung von Postern zu aktuellen Projekten auf. Wir begrüßen die Einsendung zu Promotions- und Habilitationsprojekten. Schicken Sie uns Ihren Entwurf ebenfalls bis zum 31. August

2024. Die Projektposter werden im Vorfeld der am Abend des 12. Dezember stattfindenden Jahresfeier des ausrichtenden Zentrums mit der 15. Marburger Vorlesung zum Völkerstrafrecht als Hauptvortrag mit anschließendem Stehempfang präsentiert.

Organisiert wird die Tagung im Namen des Vorstands der Sektion Rechtssoziologie vom Internationalen Forschungs- und Dokumentationszentrum Kriegsverbrecherprozesse (ICWC) an der Philipps-Universität Marburg, vertreten durch Dr. Henning de Vries. Einsendungen bitte an:

icwc@uni-marburg.de

Verbraucher:innen in der Energiewende

Workshop 18 des Kompetenzzentrums Verbraucherforschung der Verbraucherzentrale NRW e. V. (KVF NRW) mit dem Institut für Verbraucherwissenschaften (IfV) am 18. November 2024 an der Heinrich-Heine-Universität Düsseldorf

Auch wenn der unmittelbare Preisschock in der Folge des Krieges in der Ukraine abgeflaut ist, kann nicht von einem Ende der Krise gesprochen werden. Der Klimawandel schreitet voran und macht den Ausstieg aus der fossilen Wirtschaft notwendig. Diese Energiewende wird Auswirkungen auf den Alltag der Verbraucher:innen haben. bieten.

Die Veranstaltung soll eine Plattform für den inter- und transdisziplinären Austausch und Diskussionen der Risiken und Chancen des Wandels von Energieerzeugung und -verbrauch bieten. Ziel ist es, Erkenntnisse aus unterschiedlichen für die Verbraucherwissenschaften relevanten Fachrichtungen (beispielsweise Erziehungswissenschaft, Ökonomie, Politikwissenschaft, Psychologie, Rechtswissenschaft, Sozialwissenschaft, Geschichtswissenschaft, Informatik, Marketing et cetera) zusammenzuführen. Vorschläge zu folgenden möglichen Themenschwerpunkten und Fragestellungen sind willkommen:

Verbraucher:innen und Energiemärkte

- Welchen Problemen sind Verbraucher:innen an Energiemärkten ausgesetzt?
- Wie beeinflussen Energiemärkte das Verbraucherverhalten?

- Wie entwickeln sich die Märkte für erneuerbare Energien und Technologien und welche Auswirkungen hat dies auf Verbraucher:innen?

Energiewende und gesellschaftliche Konflikte

- Welche politischen Kräfte bremsen die Energiewende und verunsichern Verbraucher:innen?
- Wie kann Aufklärung gegen Klimawandelleugnung und Populismus gegen die Energiewende gestaltet werden?
- Welche Rolle spielen die Debatten um die Klimakrise in der Verbraucherpolitik?

Die soziale Frage in der Energiewende

- Wird die soziale Ungleichheit durch die Transformationen zunehmen?
- Wie können die sozialen Folgen der Energiewende abgefedert werden?
- Welches Ausmaß hat die Energiearmut und wie kann sie abgeschafft werden?

Welche Energie wollen wir und welche bekommen wir?

- Gelingt die Energiewende und welche Probleme sind mit den erneuerbaren Energien verbunden?
- Welchen Technologien gehört die Zukunft?
- Welche Maßnahmen sind für eine sichere und saubere Energieversorgung notwendig?

Handeln und Entscheiden: Was können Verbraucher:innen tun und was nicht?

- Spielen die Verbraucher:innen überhaupt eine Rolle in der Energiewende?
- Werden neue Formen der Energieversorgung an Bedeutung gewinnen (Bürger:innen-Energie / Energie-Prosumer:innen)?
- Welchen Handlungsspielraum haben Mieter:innen, Eigentümer:innen und Hausbestitzer:innen?

Bitte senden Sie ein aussagefähiges Abstract als PDF-Datei bis zum **6. September 2024** (maximal 2.000 Zeichen inkl. Leerzeichen; Titel, Autorennamen, Kontaktdaten und Keywords zählen nicht dazu).

Bis zum 13. September 2024 erhalten Sie Nachricht über die Annahme Ihres Vorschlags. In diesem Fall werden wir Sie bitten, uns bis zum 13. November 2024 eine Präsentation (PPTX-, ODP- oder PDF-Datei) zuzusenden. Bitte beachten Sie, dass die Vorträge dieses Workshops im Open Access in unserem »Jahrbuch Konsum & Verbraucherwissenschaften« erscheinen sollen. Die Abgabe der Manuskripte (als DOCX- oder ODT-Datei) soll bis zum 7. April 2025 erfolgen.

Die Reisekosten zum Workshop werden Ihnen im Rahmen des Landesreisekostengesetzes NRW und der Allgemeine Verwaltungsvorschriften zum Landesreisekostengesetz erstattet.

Mehr Informationen sowie ein Kontaktformular zur Einreichung Ihres Vorschlags finden Sie unter https://www.verbraucherforschung.nrw/. Bei Fragen wenden Sie sich bitte an:

verbraucherforschung@verbraucherzentrale.nrw.

Der Wandel des Pilgerns im heutigen Europa. Spiritualität – Praxis – Infrastruktur

Internationale Pilgertagung der Sektion Religionssoziologie vom 11. bis 13. September 2025 in Donauwörth

Pilgern erfährt in Europa seit den 1970er Jahren einen ungeahnten Boom. Inzwischen sind in qualitativer Hinsicht etliche markante Veränderungen, ja sogar Brüche zu verzeichnen. Um diese für das religiös-spirituelle und weltanschauliche Feld in Europa höchst aufschlussreiche Phänomene zu erkunden, laden wir zu einer dreitägigen Tagung nach Donauwörth, einem jahrhundertealten Wallfahrts- und Pilgerzentrum, ein. Es sollen religionssoziologische Fragestellungen samt ihrer Schnittstellen zu psychologischen, theologischen und touristischen Perspektiven ausgelotet werden.

Die Tagung findet im Rahmen der 5. Donauwörther Pilgertage statt. Veranstalter sind die Sektion Religionssoziologie in Kooperation mit der Städtischen Tourist-Information Donauwörth/Vhs und weiteren Unterstützern aus der Pilgerszene. Durch Responses werden die Fachbeiträge in die weitere Forschung eingebettet und ihre Bedeutung für die Praxis erschlossen. Dies ermöglicht Forschenden, ihre Kontakte zum Feld auszubauen.

Themen

Pilgern ist im Wandel. Nach einigen Jahrzehnten des Pilgerbooms ist es an der Zeit, Kontinuitäten, Entwicklungen und Umbrüche besonders in den Blick zu nehmen. Mögliche Fragestellungen der Beiträge können sein:

- Das weltanschauliche Profil heutiger Pilger*innen: Wie lassen sie sich in religiöser, spiritueller, soziokultureller und sozialstruktureller Hinsicht beschreiben? Was motiviert sie? Welche Unterschiede lassen sich diesbezüglich zwischen den Herkunftsländern der Pilger*innen feststellen?
- Wie verändert sich die Praxis des Pilgerns, also die Handlungsform seiner Durchführung, das Erfahren, Erleben und die Sinndeutung der Pilgernden? Welche Theorien eignen sich am besten dazu, diese Veränderungen zu verstehen und zu erklären?
- Welche Typisierungen, z.B. hinsichtlich der Art der Spiritualität und Religiosität, der biografischen Verortung und der Milieuzugehörigkeit, erweisen sich als hilfreich für das Verständnis der Vielfalt der Pilger*innen? Inwiefern müssen diese Typisierungen weiterentwickelt werden?
- Welche Forschungsmethoden erweisen sich als fruchtbar und welche Indikatoren und Dimensionen sollten verstärkte Aufmerksamkeit bekommen? Wie sind empirische und hermeneutische Herangehensweisen ins Spiel zu bringen?
- Wie entwickelt sich die Kommunikation der Pilgernden und über diese Praxis? Welche visuellen und sprachlichen Formen prägen die Diskurse und welchen Stellenwert erhalten dabei *Social Media* und Netzwerke sowie die Darstellungen institutioneller Akteure?
- Welche positiven und negativen Bewertungen des Pilgerns zirkulieren und wie verändern sich solche Zuschreibungen? In welchen Kontexten propagieren welche Akteure die jeweiligen Bewertungen?
- Wie entwickelt sich die Infrastruktur des Pilgerns (Wege, Ziele, Unterkünfte, Pilgerbegleitung, Pilgerangebote …)? Welche Profit- und Nonprofit-Akteure werden hierbei aktiv? Welche Werte und Interessen leiten sie und mit welchen Wirkungen?
- Wie wirkt sich die kulturelle, religiöse und weltanschauliche Vielfalt auf das Pilgern aus – sind doch insbesondere auf populären Pilgerwegen höchst unterschiedliche Leute unterwegs?
- Was geschieht, wenn Pilgern mit sozialethischen Anliegen (Ökologie, Frieden, globale Gerechtigkeit …) gerahmt oder für Rehabilitations-, Resozialisierungs- oder medizinische Zwecke genutzt wird?

- Können – möglicherweise nachhaltige – individuelle bzw. biografische Wirkungen des Pilgerns festgestellt werden, und wie wirken sich die jüngeren Pilgertrends aus?
- Wie können die am Pilgern beobachteten Veränderungen meso- und makrosoziologisch interpretiert werden? Welche soziologischen Theorien vermögen das Pilgern erkenntnisförderlich zu begreifen?

Für Hauptvorträge haben bislang Nurit Stadler (Jerusalem), Michael N. Ebertz (Freiburg) und Stefan Huber (Bern) zugesagt. Für die beiden Abendvorträge wurden Klaus Bieberstein (Bamberg) und Hartmut Rosa (Jena) angefragt.

Folgende Formen von Beiträgen sind erwünscht:

- Hauptvorträge (ca. 30 Min.)
- Thesenpapiere für Workshops über spezifische Fragestellungen und die Diskussion laufender Forschungsprojekte (ca. 15 Min.)
- Poster für Kurzpräsentationen und Gallery-Walk.

Bitte reichen Sie Ihr aussagekräftiges Abstract (samt Angabe des gewünschten Formats) mit bis zu 3.000 Zeichen (inkl. Leerzeichen) bis zum **1. Oktober 2024** ein. Einreichungen sind auf Deutsch oder Englisch möglich. Die Begutachtung und Mitteilung über die Annahme wird bis zum 1. Dezember 2024 abgeschlossen. Bis 31. Dezember 2024 erfolgt die Bestätigung der Annahme durch die Vortragenden. Die Programmplanung wird bis zum 31. Januar 2025 fertiggestellt. Die vergünstigte Anmeldung ist bis 1. Mai 2025 über unten angegebene Kontaktadresse möglich.

Die Tagung wird organisiert von Prof. Dr. Dr. Michael N. Ebertz (Freiburg), Dr. Michael Hainz SJ (Frankfurt Sankt Georgen), Prof. Dr. Stefan Huber (Bern) und Dr. Detlef Lienau (Freiburg).

Kontakt: pilgern@ekiba.de

Tagungen

Vulnerable Gesellschaften: Risiken und Reaktionen

Kongress der Schweizerischen Gesellschaft für Soziologie vom 9. bis 11. September 2024 an der Hochschule für Soziale Arbeit der Fachhochschule Nordwestschweiz FHNW, Campus Muttenz

Dass wir in unsicheren Zeiten leben, scheint eine soziologische Binsenwahrheit zu sein. Allerdings wurden Gesellschaften rund um den Globus in jüngster Zeit von einer außerordentlichen Häufung von akuten und persistenten Krisen und Katastrophen mit globalen Auswirkungen erschüttert wie z.B. von der Covid 19-Pandemie, dem Krieg in der Ukraine, sich beschleunigenden Effekten des Klimawandels wie Hitzewellen, Dürren und Überflutungen, von Lieferkettenunterbrüchen und Energiemangel und der massiven Zunahme von Hunger, um nur einige Stichworte zu nennen. Jede dieser Krisen stellt für sich allein schon enorme soziale, politische, ökonomische und ökologische Herausforderungen dar. Zusammengenommen erzeugen sie eine erhöhte Wahrnehmung und Betroffenheit von allgemeiner Verletzlichkeit. Vor diesem Hintergrund ist Vulnerabilität zu einem breit verwendeten Begriff in öffentlichen und politischen Diskursen geworden. In aller Regel wird er nicht lediglich deskriptiv verwendet – vielmehr kommt ihm gleichzeitig eine präskriptive Funktion zu. Vulnerabilität oder Fragilität festzustellen, ist unweigerlich verbunden mit dem moralischen und politischen Aufruf zu handeln, um potenziellen Schädigungen vorzubeugen oder sie zu mildern und soziale Ungerechtigkeiten zu beseitigen. Eine soziale Gruppe als »vulnerabel« zu charakterisieren, impliziert die Zuschreibung eines speziellen Bedarfs an Schutz und Unterstützung. Vulnerabilität wird mit einer breiten Palette von physischen, sozialen, ökonomischen oder kulturellen Faktoren, Bedingungen und Prozessen in Verbindung gebracht. In der einschlägigen Literatur werden nicht nur Menschen als verletzlich betrachtet. Der Terminus findet auch Anwendung für die Gefährdung von technischen

Infrastrukturen und ökologischen, ökonomischen, politischen und gesellschaftlichen Systemen. Entsprechend ist Vulnerabilität zum Gegenstand verschiedener akademischer Disziplinen geworden: von Medizin bis Katastrophenforschung, Ökologie, Philosophie, Psychologie, Gerontologie und Pädagogik, Recht oder Sozialer Arbeit. Was also könnten genuin soziologische Perspektiven und Beiträge zur Analyse von Vulnerabilität sein?

Im Rahmen des Kongresses soll der Begriff der Vulnerabilität in seiner Bedeutung für die soziologische Theoriebildung und Forschung kritisch sondiert werden. Zum einen wird er systematisch mit verwandten und in der Soziologie fest verankerten konzeptionellen Begriffen wie Risiko, Ungewissheit, Krise oder Prekarität respektive zu Gegenbegriffen wie Resilienz, Agency, Anpassung u.ä. in Beziehung gesetzt. Zum anderen gilt es, anhand empirischer Studien aus unterschiedlichen Feldern den gegenwärtigen Stellenwert sowie das Potenzial des Konzepts der Vulnerabilität für die soziologische Forschung zu reflektieren. Was sind die Ursachen, Formen und Folgen von Vulnerabilität? Wie reagieren Individuen, Gruppen, Organisationen, soziale Bewegungen, Staaten oder supranationale Organisationen auf unterschiedliche Formen von Vulnerabilität? Schließlich sollen die politischen und praktischen Erträge der soziologischen Analyse von Vulnerabilität ausgelotet werden.

Der Kongress wird dreisprachig auf Deutsch, Französisch und Englisch durchgeführt.

Kongressorganisation:
sgs.sozialearbeit@fhnw.ch

Norbert Elias in der Praxis. Von der Menschenwissenschaft zur Anwendung

Tagung an der Hochschule Esslingen am 20. und 21. September 2024

Das Ziel von Norbert Elias war die theoretische und begriffliche Weiterentwicklung der Menschenwissenschaften – hin zu einem konsequenten interdisziplinären Prozess- und Verflechtungsdenken. Damit eröffnete er wegweisende Perspektiven, und zwar auch in der anwendungsorientierten Forschung sowie der konkreten praktischen Anwendung. Diese greifen auf seine Konzepte und Schlüsselbegriffe zurück – ob Machtbalancen, Figurationen beziehungsweise Beziehungsgeflechte, Etablierten-Außenseiter-Beziehungen, Balancen von Fremd- und Selbstzwang, Wandel von Hierarchien in Arbeitsbeziehungen, Geschlechterbeziehungen oder Schübe von Zivilisierung und Dezivilisierung.

Die erste Anwendung entstand bereits ab den 1940er Jahren: das von SH Foulkes in Zusammenarbeit mit Elias entwickelte Modell der gruppenanalytischen Psychotherapie. Bis heute wird das Potenzial des Prozess- und Figurationsansatzes in der anwendungsorientierten Forschung und der konkreten Anwendung genutzt und weiterentwickelt, ob in Gruppenanalyse, Organisationsberatung, Kindergarten oder Sozialer Arbeit.

Ein Überblick über die vielfältigen Anwendungen des Prozess- und Figurationsansatzes in Forschung und Praxis ist nur schwer zu gewinnen. Ziel dieser Tagung ist es daher, Anwendungsideen und -ansätze aus unterschiedlichen wissenschaftlichen Disziplinen und Praxisfeldern vorzustellen und zu den gesammelten Erfahrungen miteinander in Austausch zu kommen. Schlüsselfragen hierzu können sein:

- In welchen Bereichen werden Ansätze von Elias für die praktische Anwendung als nützlich beurteilt?
- Wo finden Ansätze von Elias einen konkreten Anwendungsbezug?
- Welche Perspektiven künftiger Anwendungsbezüge lassen sich erkennen?

Die Tagung soll mit Kurzvorträgen gerahmt werden und Zeit für Fragen, Diskussionen, Austausch und geselliges Beisammensein bieten. Die Anmeldung zur Teilnahme an der Tagung hat im Juni 2024 begonnen. Tagungsgebühren werden nicht erhoben.

Kontakt:

Prof. Dr. Wolfgang Stadel, Hochschule Esslingen
E-Mail: wolfgang.stadel@hs-esslingen.de

Dr. Désirée Waterstradt, Norbert Elias Foundation
E-Mail: desiree.waterstradt@norbert-elias.com

Interdisziplinäre Antisemitismusforschung

Tagung vom 8. bis 10. Oktober 2024 an der Universität Trier

Die Tagung widmet sich gegenwärtigen und historischen Erscheinungsformen des Antisemitismus und will einen Beitrag zur kritischen Auseinandersetzung mit gegenwärtigen und historischen Erscheinungsformen des Antisemitismus leisten.

Die alle zwei Jahre stattfindenden »Nachwuchstagungen für interdisziplinäre Antisemitismusforschung« tragen der Notwendigkeit Rechnung, Antisemitismus nicht nur als Phänomen der Vergangenheit zu beleuchten, sondern auch in seiner Aktualität und seinem Bedrohungspotential zu thematisieren.

Dieses Bedrohungspotential hat sich mit den Angriffen der Hamas auf Israel am 7. Oktober 2023 erneut in seine mörderische Praxis übersetzt und einmal mehr offenbart, dass jüdisches Leben jederzeit durch den Vernichtungsdrang islamistischer Terrororganisationen, aber auch durch Staaten wie den Iran und antisemitische Akteur:innen weltweit bedroht wird und selbst der israelische Staat als Refugium für Jüdinnen und Juden keinen vollständigen Schutz vor antisemitischen Pogromen bieten kann.

Die »genozidale Botschaft« (Dan Diner) der Hamas an Jüdinnen und Juden auf der ganzen Welt macht nicht nur eine Solidarisierung mit allen von Antisemitismus Betroffenen notwendig, sondern auch eine intensive, tiefgreifende und vielschichtige wissenschaftliche Auseinandersetzung mit dem Phänomen des Antisemitismus.

Aus diesem Grund soll unsere Tagung durch aus der Nachwuchswissenschaft kommende, neue Forschungsimpulse in Verbindung mit einer fachübergreifenden Aufstellung der Referent:innen innovative Zugänge zur Antisemitismusforschung ermöglichen und Antisemitismus ganzheitlich in den Blick nehmen. Dementsprechend ist es Anspruch der Tagung, neue Ansätze zur Antisemitismusforschung zu verbreiten, den Ideenaustausch und die Netzwerkbildung unter den Teilnehmer:innen zu fördern und die Rolle von Nachwuchswissenschaftler:innen zu stärken.

Die dreitägige internationale Tagung findet in Kooperation mit der Forschungs- und Dokumentationsstelle SEAL (Universität Trier), der Beauftragten der Ministerpräsidentin für jüdisches Leben und Antisemitismusfragen des Landes Rheinland-Pfalz Monika Fuhr, dem Arbeitskreis »Erinnerung der Großregion« e.V., dem Landesverband der jüdischen Gemeinden von Rheinland-Pfalz, dem Jungen Forum der Deutsch-Israelischen Gesellschaft und dem jüdischen Studierendenverband Rheinland-Pfalz/Saarland

»Hinenu« in Trier statt. Zivilgesellschaftliche Akteur:innen werden während der Tagung die Möglichkeit haben, ihre Inhalte an Ständen zu präsentieren.

Kontakt:
iia@uni-trier.de

»Wer schützt hier eigentlich wen?«

Online-Zwischentagung des Forschungsverbunds GERDEA zum institutionellen Umgang mit rechten Angriffen gegen die Wissenschaft am 9. Oktober 2024 von 9:30 bis 17 Uhr

Eine Verschiebung der Debattenkultur nach rechts geht auch an den Hochschulen nicht vorbei. Als Akteur:innen im politischen Raum positionierten sich verschiedene Universitäten und hochschulpolitische Verbände in den letzten Monaten gegen Antisemitismus und rechte Abschiebungsfantasien. Zugleich sind die Hochschulen selbst und mit ihnen einzelne Forschende immer wieder im Fokus rechter Angriffe. Im Zuge der Corona-Pandemie haben diese Angriffe ein neues Ausmaß erfahren: Forschende selbst und wissenschaftliche Institutionen gerieten zum Feindbild in Protesten gegen staatliche Maßnahmen. In den Protestformaten mischte sich eine allgemeine Skepsis bis Feindlichkeit gegenüber wissenschaftlichen Erkenntnissen in demokratiegefährdender Weise mit antisemitischen Verschwörungsfantasien gegenüber einer ›kosmopolitischen Elite‹ aus Politik, Medien und Wissenschaft.

Zeitgleich verschärfen sich auch wissenschaftspolitisch Debatten, die schon länger brodeln: In Auseinandersetzungen um die gesellschaftspolitische Verantwortung von Forschung und Lehre werden Vorwürfe einer angeblichen ›Cancel Culture‹ erhoben; Forschende unterschiedlicher Disziplinen sehen sich mit dem Vorwurf einer angeblich ideologischen Forschungstätigkeit (›Gender-Ideologie‹) und dem Verbot geschlechtergerechter Sprache ausgesetzt. Ähnlich wie bei den Protesten im Zuge der Corona-Pandemie erfolgen die Angriffe nicht allein aus einer organisierten extremen Rechten heraus, sondern durch ein heterogenes Feld an Einzelpersonen, Gruppen und sozialen Milieus unterschiedlicher politischer Orientierungen – auch aus dem Hochschulkontext selbst.

Die mitunter polemisch geführten Debatten um eine ›Cancel-Culture‹ und ein Verbot geschlechtergerechter Sprache sorgen ebenso wie die offenen Angriffe gegen Wissenschaftler:innen für eine Verunsicherung unter Forschenden und Lehrenden, die eine Reaktion von Seiten der Institutionen notwendig erscheinen lassen. Wenn die oben beschriebenen Angriffe auf einen von Abhängigkeiten geprägten Raum treffen, wie etwa im Kontext Wissenschaft, besteht die Gefahr, dass Forschende individuelle Umgangsstrategien entwickeln (müssen), weil sie die institutionelle Rückendeckung nicht einfordern können. Vielfach fehlt es an Sensibilität, Wissen und Handlungskonzepten für Gefahrensituationen in den wissenschaftlichen Einrichtungen. Oft wird aber auch den Wissenschaftler:innen selbst erst spät im Forschungsprozess bewusst, welchen Anfeindungen sie in der Forschungspraxis ausgesetzt sein können. Angemessene Gegenmaßnahmen werden demnach mitunter zu spät ergriffen. Während einige Forschungsinstitutionen bereits institutionelle Schutzkonzepte und Handlungsempfehlungen erarbeitet haben, stehen andere Einrichtungen etwaigen Initiativen zum Schutz ihrer Mitarbeitenden verhalten gegenüber. Die oben genannten Angriffe richten sich nicht zuletzt auch gegen Studierende, Doktorand:innen und freie Lehrbeauftragte, die sich nicht auf die Fürsorgepflicht der Universität als Arbeitgeber berufen können.

Vor diesem Hintergrund möchten wir die jüngeren öffentlich geführten Debatten um Angriffe gegen Wissenschaftler:innen ergänzen um den Blick auf institutionelle Schutzkonzepte und Handlungsempfehlungen. Die Tagungsthemen können sich folgenden Fragen widmen:

- Wen treffen die Angriffe? Gibt es Felder und/oder Disziplinen, die stärker als andere involviert sind in wissenschaftspolitische und/oder wissenschaftsfeindliche Debatten und Angriffe? Welche weiterführende Forschung braucht es?
- Welche Fragen stellen sich für Schutzkonzepte wissenschaftlicher Einrichtungen? Welche Perspektiven fehlen bislang, auch in der Debatte um und Forschung zu Schutzkonzepten?
- Gibt es gelungene Beispiele, bei denen sich wissenschaftliche oder nichtwissenschaftliche Institutionen langfristig ihrer gesellschaftlichen Verantwortung stellen und den damit einhergehenden Angriffen auf ihre Arbeit frühzeitig begegnen? Welche Instrumente waren hier hilfreich?
- Welche Rolle spielt das Recht in der Auseinandersetzung mit rechten Hatestorms oder Unterlassungsaufforderungen gegen Wissenschaftler:innen und wissenschaftliche Institutionen?

- Welche Forderungen können gegenüber Förderinstitutionen von wissenschaftlichen Einrichtungen und freien Trägern (z.B. DFG, Stiftungen, Ministerien) formuliert werden?
- Wie können Kooperationen zwischen Hochschulen und außer-universitären Institutionen aussehen?
- Welche Erfahrungen praktischer Solidarität sind bereits gemacht worden? Welche Rolle können Fachgesellschaften, Gewerkschaften und andere Netzwerke spielen?

Die Online-Tagung wird ausgerichtet vom Forschungsverbund GERDEA (»Wechselwirkungen zwischen gesellschaftlichen Geschlechterverhältnissen und der zeitgenössischen extremen Rechten. Dynamiken – Effekte – Ambivalenzen«). Am Verbund beteiligt sind die Forschungseinrichtungen Frankfurt University of Applied Sciences, Justus-Liebig-Universität Gießen, Philipps-Universität Marburg und Dissens e.V. – Institut für Bildung und Forschung Berlin sowie als Praxispartner:innen der Bundesverband Frauenberatungsstellen und Frauennotrufe Frauen gegen Gewalt e.V., der Bundesverband Mobile Beratung e.V., das Paritätische Bildungswerk Bundesverband e.V., der Bundesverband Jungen*arbeit sowie Gesicht zeigen! Für ein weltoffenes Deutschland e.V.

Kontakt:

Viktoria Rösch, Frankfurt University of Applied Sciences
E-Mail: viktoria.roesch@m4.fra-uas.de und

Juliane Lang, Universität Gießen
E-Mail: juliane.lang@uni-giessen.de

Babyboomer.
Sozialräumliche Perspektiven auf die Vielen

Tagung der Rheinland-Pfälzischen Technischen Universität Kaiserslautern-Landau, Fachgebiet Stadtsoziologie am 14. Oktober 2024

In der Konferenz adressieren wir die geburtenstarken Jahrgänge 1955 bis 1969 (»Babyboomer«). Mit dem sukzessiven Übergang der Babyboomer in den Ruhestand sind die Gesellschaft und insbesondere die Kommunen gefordert, angemessene Angebote zum Wohnen und für Betätigungen zu entwickeln.

Ziel der Konferenz ist es, sich datengestützt und auf empirischer Basis über Babyboomer in verschiedenen Lebenssituationen auszutauschen. Wir diskutieren hier die Lebensformen, Arbeit, Wohnen und Freizeit aus nationaler und internationaler Perspektive.

Die Tagung steht im Kontext des interdisziplinären Projekts *Ageing Smart*, das Angebote, Erreichbarkeiten und Perspektiven der Babyboomer in verschiedenen Modellkommunen analysiert, um Planungen vor Ort zu unterstützen. Es wird gefördert von der Carl-Zeiss-Stiftung und RPTU Kaiserslautern-Landau.

Als Vorträge sind geplant:
- Stadt-Land Unterschiede in der sozialen und politischen Teilhabe der Babyboomer (Julia Simonson)
- Erwerbsarbeit im späteren Erwachsenenalter (Andreas Mergenthaler)
- Persönliche Netzwerke (Lea Ellwardt)
- Wohnen und Ortsbindung (Andreas Hartung/ Benjamin Stefan)
- Ehrenamtliches Engagement der Babyboomer (Claudia Vogel)
- Babyboomer in der Schweiz: Mythen und Realitäten des Wohnens (Nicola Hilti/ Christian Reutlinger)
- Babyboomer International (Karina Pallagst)
- Kommunalfinanzen: Bedeutung des Wechsels in den Ruhestand (Martin Junkernheinrich)
- Babyboomer ante portas: Chancen und Herausforderungen für Kommunen (Karin Haist)
- Babyboomer als literarischer Gegenstand (Rainer Furch / Madeleine Giese)

Die Tagung findet von 9 bis 17 Uhr in der Station Lounge, Am Hauptbahnhof 10 in 60329 Frankfurt statt. Bei Fragen wenden Sie sich bitte an:

Prof. Dr. Annette Spellerberg
E-Mail: annette.spellerberg@ru.rptu.de

Wir bitten um Anmeldung bei

Maximilian Henzel
E-Mail: maximilian.henzel@ru.rptu.de

Prof. em. Juan E. Corradi, New York University, Dep. of Sociology, 383 Lafayette Street, New York, NY 10003, USA, E-Mail: juancorradi @gmail.com

Dr. Jördis Grabow, Georg-August-Universität Göttingen, Institut für Diversitätsforschung, Platz der Göttinger Sieben 3, D-37073 Göttingen, E-Mail: joerdis.grabow@uni-goettingen.de

Prof. Dr. Corinna Kleinert, Leibniz-Institut für Bildungsverläufe (LIfBi), Wilhelmsplatz 3, D-96047 Bamberg, E-Mail: corinna.kleinert@lifbi.de

Prof. Dr. Hubert Knoblauch, Technische Universität Berlin, Institut für Soziologie, Fraunhoferstraße 33-36, D-10587 Berlin, E-Mail: Knoblauch@tu-berlin.de

Linn-Sophie Löber, M.A., Philipps-Universität Marburg, Internationales Forschungs- und Dokumentationszentrum Kriegsverbrecherprozesse (ICWC), Universitätsstraße 7, D-35032 Marburg, E-Mail: linn-sophie.loeber@uni-marburg.de

Prof. Dr. Helma Lutz, Goethe Universität Frankfurt am Main, Fachbereich 03 Gesellschaftswissenschaften, Theodor-W.-Adorno-Platz 6, D-60323 Frankfurt am Main, E-Mail: lutz@soz.uni-frankfurt.de

Prof. Dr. Anika Oettler, Philipps-Universität Marburg, Institut für Soziologie, Ketzerbach 11, D-35032 Marburg, E-Mail: oettler@staff.uni-marburg.de

Dr. Clara Ruvituso, Ibero-Amerikanisches Institut, Potsdamer Straße 37, D-10785 Berlin, E-Mail: ruvituso@iai.spk-berlin.de

Dr. Fabio Santos, Freie Universität Berlin, Lateinamerika-Institut, Rüdesheimer Straße 54-56, D-14197 Berlin, E-Mail: fabio.santos@fu-berlin.de

Kristina Schäfer, M.A., Johannes Keppler Universität, Institut für Soziologie, Altenberger Straße 69, A-4040 Linz, E-Mail: kristina.schaefer@jku.at

Dr. Miriam Friz Trzeciak, BTU Cottbus-Senftenberg, Fakultät 5 – Wirtschaft, Recht und Gesellschaft, Erich-Weinert-Straße 1, D-03046 Cottbus, E-Mail: Miriam.Trzeciak@b-tu.de

Prof. Dr. Georg Vobruba, Universität Leipzig, Institut für Soziologie, Beethovenstraße 15, D-04107 Leipzig, E-Mail: vobruba@uni-leipzig.de

Dr. Mathias Wagner, Leibniz Universität Hannover, Institut für Soziologie, Schneiderberg 50, D-30167 Hannover, E-Mail: postbox.mathias.wagner@web.de

Juan E. Corradi
The End of Sociology?

Der Autor analysiert den Status der Soziologie aus der persönlichen Perspektive von mehr als fünfzig Jahren Forschung und Lehre auf diesem Gebiet. Er beobachtet den relativen Niedergang der Disziplin in drei Dimensionen: Theorie, empirische Studien und berufliche Beschäftigung. Er stellt eine Verlagerung von der Objektivität zur Lobbyarbeit fest, eine Entwicklung, die die Soziologie anfällig für politische Angriffe macht – vor allem durch rechte Politiker und Bewegungen in den USA und darüber hinaus.

The author analyses the status of sociology from the personal perspective of more than fifty years researching and teaching in the field. He observes the relative decline of the discipline in three dimensions: theory, empirical studies, and professional employment. He detects a shift from objectivity to advocacy, a development that makes it vulnerable to political attacks – mostly from right-wing politicians and movements in the US and beyond.

Georg Vobruba
Soziologische Spuren im Verschwörungsdenken

Soziologie und Verschwörungsdenken haben den Anspruch gemeinsam, die sozialen Verhältnisse zu erklären. Allerdings unternehmen sie das im Rahmen diametral entgegengesetzter Logiken. Die Soziologie bietet relationale Erklärungen an, im Verschwörungsweltbild dagegen wird alles auf die bösen Intentionen eines mächtiges Handlungszentrums zurückgeführt. Dies bringt dem Verschwörungsdenken Erklärungsprobleme, die es durch Lügenvorwürfe und das Behaupten von Gegenwahrheiten zu neutralisieren versucht. Dadurch freilich wird eine Dynamik in Gang gesetzt, in der dem Verschwörungsdenken die Wirklichkeit Schritt für Schritt verloren geht. Diese Dynamik wird in dem Beitrag rekonstruiert, um der Frage nach Ähnlichkeiten zwischen Verschwörungsdenken und Soziologie sowie deren Ursachen nachzugehen. Ergebnis sind einerseits soziologisch informierte Einsichten in die Dynamik von Lügen und Wirklichkeitsverweigerung, andererseits Spuren soziologischer Argumentationen im Verschwörungsdenken, die zu soziologischer Selbstreflexion anregen sollten.

Sociology and conspiracy thinking claim to explain society in common. However, they do so within the framework of diametrically opposed logics. Sociology offers relational explanations, whereas in the conspiracy worldview, everything is attributed to the evil intentions of a powerful center of action. This creates explanatory problems for conspiracy thinking, which it attempts to neutralize by accusing the mainstream of lying and by asserting counter-truths. However, this sets in motion a dynamic in which conspiracy thinking gradually loses touch with reality. This dynamic is reconstructed in the article in order to pursue the question of similarities between conspiracy thinking and sociology as well as their causes. The results are, on the one hand, sociologically informed insights into the dynamics of lies and the denial of reality and, on the other hand, traces of sociological argumentation in conspiracy thinking, which should encourage sociological self-reflection.

Anika Oettler, Clara Ruvituso, Fabio Santos
Dekolonisierung als Dekanonisierung?

Der Beitrag greift die jüngst auch in der SOZIOLOGIE geführten Debatten zur Öffnung und Dekolonisierung des Kanons und des Fachs auf und erweitert sie durch einen Blick auf die Geschichte der deutschsprachigen Soziologie und Lateinamerikaforschung, inklusive ihrer Austauschbeziehungen mit lateinamerikanischen und karibischen Intellektuellen: Exemplarisch dienen uns hierfür die gegenwärtige, späte und ausgewählte Rezeption Aníbal Quijanos sowie die (in Vergessenheit geratene) produktive Rezeption der *Dependencia*-Ansätze in den 1970er und 1980er Jahren in der spezifischen bundesdeutschen akademischen Landschaft. Mit dieser fachgeschichtlichen Rekonstruktion und Re-Lektüre soziologischer Theorie argumentieren wir, dass die gegenwärtige Beschränkung der hiesigen Soziologie auf nordwesteuropäische und nordamerikanische Kontexte historisch keine Konstante darstellt und deshalb mit Blick auf die Zukunft durchaus veränderbar ist.

The article takes up the recent debates in SOZIOLOGIE on the opening and decolonization of the canon and the discipline, expanding on them by taking a close look at the history of German sociology and Latin American Studies, including its relations of exchange with Latin American and Caribbean intellectuals: Our exemplary case studies are the current, belated, and selective reception of Aníbal Quijano as well as the (forgotten) productive reception of *dependencia* approaches in the 1970s and 1980s in the specific German academic landscape. With this historical reconstruction and re-reading of sociological theory, we argue that the current focus of German sociology on Northwestern European and North American contexts is not a historical constant and can therefore be changed in the future.

Mathias Wagner
Benötigt qualitative Forschung eine schriftliche Absicherung der Ethik?

In der qualitativen Sozialforschung wird heute die schriftliche Zustimmung der Interviewpartnerinnen und -partner zu Interviews gefordert. Bis vor wenigen Jahren reichte dagegen noch die Selbstverpflichtung der Wissenschaftlerinnen und Wissenschaftler zur Anonymisierung der Daten und zum Persönlichkeitsschutz der Akteure aus. Es wird die Frage aufgeworfen, ob mit der Veränderung zur schriftlichen Form tendenziell bestimmte soziale Gruppen die Teilnahme an Forschungen aus Misstrauen verweigern. Trifft das zu, so wird der Zugang zu vulnerablen sozialen Schichten oder zu Personen mit Misstrauen gegenüber der etablierten Gesellschaft unmöglich. Zudem widerspricht die schriftliche Zustimmung zu einem Interview der Alltagslogik von Vertrauen in der Kommunikation. Gerade in ethnografischen Forschungen gewähren Akteure aufgrund von nicht formalen Kriterien Einblick in ihren Alltag.

In qualitative social research today, the written consent of interviewees is required for interviews. Until a few years ago, however, the self-commitment of the researchers to anonymize the data and to protect the privacy of the participants was sufficient. The question is raised as to whether the change to the written form means that certain social groups tend to refuse to participate in research out of mistrust. If this is the case, access to vulnerable social groups or people with a mistrust of established society becomes impossible. In addition, written consent to an interview contradicts the everyday logic of trust in communication. In ethnographic research in particular, actors provide insight into their everyday lives on the basis of non-formal criteria.

Bitte berücksichtigen Sie folgende Hinweise zur Textgestaltung:

Verwenden Sie *Fußnoten* nur für inhaltliche Kommentare, nicht für bibliographische Angaben. Geben Sie *Literaturhinweise im Text* durch Nennung des Autorennamens, des Erscheinungsjahres und ggf. der Seitenzahl in Klammern. Zum Beispiel (König 1962: 17).

Bei *bis zu drei Autor:innen* geben Sie alle Namen an und trennen durch Kommata; bei *mehr als drei Autor:innen* ergänzen Sie den ersten Namen um »et al.«. Kennzeichnen Sie *mehrere Titel pro Autor:in* und Erscheinungsjahr durch Hinzufügung von a, b, c … (König 1962a, 1962b).

Mehrere, aufeinander folgende Literaturhinweise werden durch Semikolon getrennt (König 1962: 64; Berger, Luckmann 1974: 137)

In der *Literaturliste am Schluss des Manuskriptes* führen Sie alle zitierten Titel alphabetisch nach Autorennamen und je Autor:in nach Erscheinungsjahr (aufsteigend) geordnet auf, bei mehreren Autor:innen alle namentlich durch Schrägstrich getrennt nennen. Geben Sie Verlagsort und Verlag an.

Bücher: Luhmann, Niklas 1984: Soziale Systeme. Grundriss einer allgemeinen Theorie. Frankfurt am Main: Suhrkamp.

Zeitschriftenbeiträge: Müller-Benedict, Volker 2003: Modellierung in der Soziologie – heutige Fragestellungen und Perspektiven. SOZIOLOGIE, 32. Jg., Heft 1, 21–36.

Beiträge aus Sammelbänden: Lutz, Helma 2003: Leben in der Twilightzone. In Jutta Allmendinger (Hg.), Entstaatlichung und soziale Sicherheit. Opladen: Leske + Budrich, 254–266.

Internetquellen: Stark, Philip B. / Freishtat, Richard 2014: An Evaluation of Course Evaluations. ScienceOpen Research, doi: 10.14293/S2199-1006.1.SOREDU.AOFRQA.v1.

oder Steffen, Wiebke 2003: Polizeilich registrierte Gewalttaten junger Menschen: Grund zu Furcht und Sorge? Sozialwissenschaften und Berufspraxis, 26. Jg., Heft 2, 135–148. https://nbn-resolving.org/urn:nbn:de:0168-ssoar-38044. Letzter Aufruf am 27. April 2021.

Im Literaturverwaltungsprogramm *Citavi* können Sie unseren *Zitationsstil »Soziologie – Forum der Deutschen Gesellschaft für Soziologie«* nutzen. Fügen Sie Ihrem Manuskript bitte eine *deutsche* und eine *englische Zusammenfassung von maximal je 15 Zeilen*, sowie *Name, Titel* und *Korrespondenzadresse* bei. Schicken Sie Ihren Text bitte als .docx, .rtf oder .odt per E-Mail an die Redaktion der SOZIOLOGIE: soz-red@sozio.uni-leipzig.de.

Für *Berichte aus den Sektionen* beachten Sie bitte, dass der Text 7.500 Zeichen (inkl. Leerzeichen) nicht überschreiten sollte.